Cambridge E

Elements in Forensic
edited by
Tim Grant
Aston University
Tammy Gales
Hofstra University

LEGAL–LAY DISCOURSE AND PROCEDURAL JUSTICE IN FAMILY AND COUNTY COURTS

Tatiana Grieshofer
Birmingham City University

CAMBRIDGE
UNIVERSITY PRESS

C000129295

CAMBRIDGE
UNIVERSITY PRESS

Shaftesbury Road, Cambridge CB2 8EA, United Kingdom

One Liberty Plaza, 20th Floor, New York, NY 10006, USA

477 Williamstown Road, Port Melbourne, VIC 3207, Australia

314–321, 3rd Floor, Plot 3, Splendor Forum, Jasola District Centre, New Delhi – 110025, India

103 Penang Road, #05–06/07, Visioncrest Commercial, Singapore 238467

Cambridge University Press is part of Cambridge University Press & Assessment, a department of the University of Cambridge.

We share the University's mission to contribute to society through the pursuit of education, learning and research at the highest international levels of excellence.

www.cambridge.org
Information on this title: www.cambridge.org/9781009486927

DOI: 10.1017/9781009378031

First published 2024

A catalogue record for this publication is available from the British Library.

ISBN 978-1-009-48692-7 Hardback
ISBN 978-1-009-37799-7 Paperback
ISSN 2634-7334 (online)
ISSN 2634-7326 (print)

Legal–Lay Discourse and Procedural Justice in Family and County Courts

Elements in Forensic Linguistics

DOI: 10.1017/9781009378031
First published online: March 2024

Tatiana Grieshofer
Birmingham City University

Author for correspondence: Tatiana Grieshofer, tatiana.grieshofer@bcu.ac.uk

Abstract: Focusing on adversarial legal settings, this Element explores discursive practices in court proceedings which often involve unrepresented parties – private family proceedings and small claims cases. Such proceedings present the main caseload of county and family courts but pose immense challenges when it comes to legal–lay communication. Drawing on court observations, alongside textual and interview data, the Element pursues three aims: (1) developing the methodological and theoretical framework for exploring discursive practices in legal settings; (2) establishing the link between legal–lay discourse and procedural justice; (3) presenting and contextualising linguistic phenomena as an inherent part of court research and practice. The Element illustrates how linguistic input can contribute to procedural changes and court reforms across different adversarial and non-adversarial legal settings. The exploration of discursive practices embedded in court processes and procedures consolidates and advances the existing court research conducted within the fields of socio-legal studies and forensic and legal linguistics. This title is also available as Open Access on Cambridge Core.

Keywords: family courts, county courts, legal–lay discourse, procedural justice, self-represented litigants

ISBNs: 9781009486927 (HB), 9781009377997 (PB), 9781009378031 (OC)
ISSNs: 2634-7334 (online), 2634-7326 (print)

Contents

Series Preface   1

Author Preface: For Forensic and Legal Linguists   1

Author Preface: For Legal Scholars   3

1 Introduction   4

2 Legal–Lay Discourse   7

3 Discourse of Civil and Family Proceedings   12

4 Discursive Practices, Procedural Justice and Legal
  Participation   16

5 Language Data and Empirical Methods   21

6 Discursive Practices in Child Arrangement Proceedings   25

7 Discursive Practices in Financial Remedy Proceedings   40

8 Discursive Practices in County Courts   48

9 Concluding Thoughts and Future Directions   55

Appendix: Court Observations Template   61

References   63

Series Preface

The Elements in Forensic Linguistics series from Cambridge University Press publish across four main topic areas: (1) investigative and forensic text analysis; (2) the study of spoken linguistic practices in legal contexts; (3) the linguistic analysis of written legal texts; (4) explorations of the origins, development and scope of the field in various countries and regions. Legal–Lay Discourse and Procedural Justice in Family and County Courts by Tatiana Grieshofer is an interdisciplinary study that examines spoken and written discourse situated in the second and third categories.

As the first Element focused on legal–lay discourse, Grieshofer brings a unique perspective to the examination of discourse throughout the pre-court and courtroom stages of the legal process in child arrangements, financial remedy hearings and small claims courts. Drawing on Hymes' (1962) ethnography of communication as her primary methodological framework, which allows for an exploration of real-life situations within their socio-cultural contexts, Grieshofer is able to provide insightful qualitative and quantitative analyses of linguistic features that are contextualised within her forty courtroom observations. She further complements her ethnographic findings with personal communications from individual interviews with self-represented litigants and lawyers, quantitative data from surveys of various participants throughout the legal process and genre analyses of frequently downloaded court forms related to the cases at hand. As she accurately states, this mix-methods approach allows her study 'to reflect on: lived court experiences of court users, in-court and out-of-court communication, narrativisation and elicitation practices on institutional and personal levels, systemic communication-related challenges, procedural barriers, discursive practices embedded in practice directions and procedural rules'. Grieshofer's Element successfully accomplishes these ambitious goals.

As such an in-depth study, this Element will be of benefit not only to linguists interested in lay–legal discourse but also to those advocating for best discursive practices within the procedural justice framework. We are excited to have two more Elements on lay–legal language in the pipeline to complement this exciting publication.

Tammy Gales
Series Editor

Author Preface: For Forensic and Legal Linguists

Conducting linguistic research into legal discourse and interaction is replete with challenges and opportunities. One of the main constraints for researchers is restricted access to data (cf. D'hondt and May 2022; Wright 2021). As linguists, we are interested in exploring spoken and written texts and interactions in context. Yet, it is mainly written legal discourse (e.g. legislation, judgements, contracts, media reports on major legal cases) that is readily available as part of wider public knowledge, open justice and public legal education. Access to other language data from legal proceedings, including spoken interactions, is patchy at best. Considerable work is being carried out to locate publicly available data from individual cases and databases (Gales and Wing 2022), but such data tend to be limited to court transcripts or audio/video recordings from high-profile and widely medialised cases (e.g. *Johnny Depp* v. *Amber Heard* defamation case on YouTube), experimental settings (e.g. data collected by Braun and Taylor 2012) or historical proceedings (Hitchcock et al. 2012; Linder 2023). Although such cases provide an insight into a wide range of legal and court discourses, the drawback is that they do not reflect the commonplace proceedings, in which parties tend to encounter multiple complications when accessing the justice system due to procedural, cognitive, discursive, attitudinal and practical barriers (Grieshofer 2022b; McKeever et al. 2018; Trinder et al. 2014). It is these high-volume cases in family and county courts that have so far been under-researched, predominantly due to a wide range of data access challenges.

There is nonetheless a considerable potential for linguistic research to con-tribute to enhancing access to justice by investigating diverse communicative aspects from pre-court and court stages of family and county court proceedings. One way to gain access to these cases is to conduct court observations and draw on ethnographic linguistic approaches. While research in socio-legal studies often draws on court observations to explore the impact of court interactions on access to justice (cf. Trinder et al. 2014), ethnographic methods have so far been underutilised in linguistic research. Arguably, this is because even with court permissions and data access clearances, it is only possible to make notes during court observations. For the purposes of linguistic research, it is customary to work with the recordings of actual interactions or at least verbatim transcripts transcribed following conversation analysis transcription practices (cf. Sacks et al. 1974). The notes about speech events cannot substitute audio recordings of court hearings, which could be made in the past (cf. Conley and O'Barr 1998; O'Barr 1982), but are no longer possible (see Section 5 for more information on access to language data). Nevertheless, despite the seemingly linguistically impoverished data which can be acquired during court observations, ethno-graphic methods enable researchers to explore the experiences of a high number of court users within a relatively short period of time and examine the cases through diverse analytical lenses, focusing on discursive practices, power rela-tions, turn-taking, topic management or many other aspects of interaction and communication management (cf. also D'hondt 2021).

The aspiration behind the Element is to inspire forensic linguists and language and law scholars to enter the realm of socio-legal research by (1) expanding the applications of linguistic ethnographic methods and adding to the methodological rigour of empirical court studies; (2) providing the analysis which reaches beyond the descriptive aspects of courtroom discourse and gains on relevance for the investigation of practice directions, court procedures and public and administrative law; (3) contributing to the understanding of the role of communication in procedural justice.

Author Preface: For Legal Scholars

It is widely accepted that '[f]ew professions are as concerned with language as is the law' (Tiersma 1993: 135). What is less known is the extent to which linguistics can contribute to the study and interpretation of law, legal practice and socio-legal research more widely. Language and communication play a crucial role in legal proceedings as trials are conducted, framed and inter-preted through linguistic performances – spoken and written interactions and texts. It is through these linguistic performances that the court participants' characters and narratives are construed and evaluated for credibility; linguists can therefore contribute a critical insight into understanding how justice is delivered or denied (cf. Luchjenbroers and Aldridge 2008: 191).

Linguistic research is of special significance to the proceedings in lower courts where accessing legal advice and representation is often problematic for the parties (Maclean and Eekelaar 2019; Moorhead and Sefton 2005; Smith et al. 2017; Trinder et al. 2014), which leads to them being particularly suscep-tible to communicative challenges and discursive disadvantages (Grieshofer 2022c; Tkacukova 2016). Much of the influential socio-legal research points to multiple language and communication issues, such as the lack of clear pre-court information, ambiguous instructions and directions in court communication or insufficient communication among statutory agencies (Hunter et al. 2020; Trinder et al. 2014). Yet, a substantial input from linguists is rarely sought, and these long-standing challenges thus keep persevering throughout different stages of the proceedings (Grieshofer 2023b).

The Element illustrates that linguistic insight is crucial for addressing a wide range of communicative, cognitive, procedural, legal and attitudinal challenges faced by court users on a daily basis. This extends beyond the typical examples of how, for instance, following plain language guidelines can contribute to enhancing the comprehensibility and readability of legal texts (Adler 2012). The language of law and the discourse of legal proceedings are inherently complex and cannot be easily made accessible through linguistic simplifications

(Assy 2011; Bhatia 2004). The Element presents a theoretical and methodo-logical innovation by introducing the importance of exploring discursive practices embedded in court processes and procedures. The focus on discursive practices enables researchers to contextualise elicitation practices, narrativisation strategies and other discursive processes as part of procedural justice and, as a result, enhance legal participation of lay court users. The Element thus aims to inspire interdisciplinary collaborations by (1) illustrating how applied linguistics can contribute to the conceptual and methodological frameworks used in court research within socio-legal studies, (2) establishing the impact court processes and procedures have on the practicalities of the court users' active engagement with the proceedings and their ability to share their stories, and (3) identifying practical solutions for enhancing procedural justice through procedural changes and court reforms.

1 Introduction

County and family courts in the jurisdiction of England and Wales adjudicate a wide range of civil and family disputes, such as small claims cases, debt, compensations for injuries, property repossessions, child arrangements, divorce and financial remedy proceedings. In 2021, there were 1,582,363 civil claims initiated and 980,474 judgements made (the majority of cases were resolved via mediation, settled out of court, dropped or did not proceed to trial for other reasons), alongside 265,676 family cases initiated and 249,985 disposed of in family courts (the statistics are collected in different ways across different types of courts, hence the numbers on judgements made vs. court disposals – *Courts Data* 2023). Civil and family proceedings thus concern many businesses, indi-viduals and families who come to court in an anticipation of having their day in court and presenting their accounts of events before the judge. The reality they are confronted with is that very little time is allocated for them to share their stories during a hearing and there are many procedural requirements they need to fulfil before they are given an opportunity to present their stories in court.

The discourse of lower courts embeds multiple communicative events and discourse types, constituting a complex nexus of genres used for eliciting and presenting evidence. As part of adversarial proceedings, the parties are expected to engage in the battle of two conflicting narratives, but what many lay people are unaware of is that presenting their case involves a multi-stage process, which follows complex court processes and procedures. The discrepancies between legal and lay narrativisation styles are well-documented and there is little doubt that the differences complicate litigants' access to justice (Conley and O'Barr 1998; O'Barr and Conley 1991). What is less known is the extent to which court processes and procedures, designed to promote fairness and facilitate due process, can take the focus away from the parties' narratives (Grieshofer 2022b, 2023b). As the cases progress through individual procedural steps, the stories that parties enter the proceedings with are constantly being reframed and reinterpreted (Coulthard and Johnson 2007) and it is common that court users leave the hearings, the outcome of which is important to them, feeling that they were not heard (Hunter et al. 2020). The judiciary and advocates, on the other hand, report being frustrated by the lack of parties' engagement with the process, missing paperwork, insufficient procedural compliance and the resulting additional work for court staff (cf. Trinder et al. 2014).

The pressures on lower courts are immense. The complexity of the current challenges faced by the parties, legal professionals and court services stems from a number of cognate contextual factors triggered by changes in the sociopolitical climate as well as the resistance to the systemic change within legal institutions and professional practice (cf. Macfarlane 2005; Hunter et al. 2020). One major obstacle is linked to the fact that, at the time of writing this, ten years have passed since the Legal Aid, Sentencing, and Punishment of Offenders Act 2012 (LASPO) came in force in 2013, which substantially cut the provision of legal aid, removing most civil and private family cases from the scope of publicly funded legal advice and representation (Maclean and Eekelaar 2019). The courts, legal professionals, judiciary and litigants found themselves in the unsettling circumstances due to the swift shift from a fairly generous legal aid provision (which in the previous decades was nonetheless deteriorating more gradually due to austerity measures; cf. Maclean and Eekelaar 2019: 6–13) to the practically non-existing support. As a result, the courts are overflowing with litigants who have to represent themselves because they cannot afford to hire an advocate or can only do so for certain tasks rather than the entirety of the proceedings. The quarterly family court statistics reports show that in 82 per cent of private hearings alone, at least one of the parties was not represented during the most recent quarter of July to September 2022, in comparison to approximately 53 per cent pre-LASPO (*Family Court Statistics Quarterly: July to September 2022*).

Self-represented litigants (SRLs) or litigants in person (LiPs), the term used in the UK jurisdictions, are thus a common feature of small claims hearings, private family proceedings and other types of cases heard in county and family courts. Yet, SRLs are expected to function within the legal system and follow court procedures which were designed by lawyers for lawyers (Ainsworth 2015; Trinder et al. 2014). Procedural aspects of adversarial proceedings tend to be very complex and resistant to change (Kessler 2004: section 1). As an inherent part of adversarialism is the right to self-represent, the jurisdiction of England and

Wales is one of many legal contexts in which SRLs experience barriers when accessing the justice system (Hough 2010; Macfarlane 2013; McKeever et al. 2018; Richardson et al. 2012). To support lay court users, many countries have been trialling different approaches and establishing a range of initiatives: self-help centres (Hough 2010); community-based centres run by law schools, professional organisations or charities (Macfarlane 2013; Maclean and Eekelaar 2019); support from lay advisers specialising in a specific legal area (e.g. Jean-Louis 2021); investing in online resources and digital solutions (Laster and Kornhauser 2017). But these remedial techniques are limited in their effectiveness, availability and type of information and advice offered. Furthermore, it is not only SRLs but also represented clients who struggle with the alienating nature of complex court procedures embedded in adversarial adjudication (cf. Hunter et al. 2020). What is becoming increasingly clear is that it is necessary to reform the system, adapting the role of the judiciary and moving away from adversarialism (Firestone and Weinstein 2004; Hunter et al. 2020; McIntosh et al. 2008).

The alternatives to adversarial proceedings include investigative models, problem-solving courts, enabling approaches and other adjudication models (Hunter et al. 2020; *Problem-solving Courts* 2023; Thomas 2012). What these innovations share is an attempt to streamline communication and adopt a more targeted and user-focused approach to disputes. Language and communication are thus at the heart of these procedural and systemic changes, but the input from linguists does not tend to be actively sought or considered as a key component of court reform programmes. Yet, many of the current difficulties with the court users' engagement can be traced back to legal–lay communication barriers and procedurally driven discursive limitations (Grieshofer 2022b, 2023b). By exploring discursive practices embedded in court processes and procedures, the Element aims to raise legal professionals' awareness of the role language and communication play in procedural justice and encourage socio-legal scholars and court reformers to collaborate with linguists on planning and implementing procedural and systemic changes.

Drawing on court observations and interview data in combination with the exploration of genres embedded in court procedures, the Element develops a theoretical framework for exploring diverse aspects of discursive practices, such as elicitation practices, narrativisation practices and information provision practices. The theoretical approach developed for exploring discursive practices allows to cover all stages of legal proceedings (including pre-court and hearing stages), categorise all communicative events and discourse types, evaluate communicative roles and performances of all participants (including litigants, lawyers, judiciary, statutory agencies, court management and administration), contextualise legal–lay communication challenges as part of court processes and procedures, and model the impact of court procedures on discursive practices and vice versa. The framework thus provides a methodological toolkit with direct applications for court research and legal practice. Given the generalisable and all-encompassing nature of the concepts discussed, the theory and methodology presented here are applicable to diverse legal settings, including adversarial and non-adversarial settings (e.g. inquisitorial legal systems). The originality of the Element thus lies in establishing a universal conceptualisation which links discursive practices to procedural justice and, in doing so, offers practical solutions for otherwise unattainable procedural justice ideals. The ambition is that in future this approach is considered as part of procedural changes and systemic court reforms.

2 Legal–Lay Discourse

Much of the evidentiary basis of legal proceedings tends to be established through different types of spoken and written legal–lay interactions (e.g. court forms, witness statements, witness examination). Legal–lay discourse is replete with challenges (cf. Heffer et al. 2013): the rule-governed legal discourse is alienating for lay people while lay narrativisation and interaction strategies do not fit with legal and procedural requirements (O'Barr 1982). The risk of communicative issues arising between legal professionals and lay participants is considerable due to distinct communicative aims, interaction rules, semantic mapping, cognitive experiences and discursive styles (Davies 2013; Rock et al. 2013: 5–8). Lay participation is, nonetheless, crucial for testing evidence and administering justice (Hans 2003) as well as an important component of the democratic legal system (Hans 2003; Malsch 2009). There is little doubt that continuous efforts to enhance the mutual comprehensibility and, when possible, make adjustments to increase the compatibility of legal–lay discursive styles should be part of the justice system (cf. Doak et al. 2021; Grieshofer 2023b; Hunter et al. 2020); the only question is how to do this best. There are different roles and stages lay people are involved in, which impacts their responsibilities and the resulting interactional space and resources available to them for contributing to legal proceedings (cf. Thornborrow 2014). In the context of county and family courts, lay people participate in legal proceedings in the following roles:

1. as those directly involved in the proceedings:
   a. parties to the proceedings represented by an advocate (claimants, litigants, respondents);
   b. self-represented parties;
   c. (expert) witnesses;
2. as public participants in the justice system:
   a. lay justices – magistrates (adversarial legal system).

The Element mainly focuses on self-represented parties as their experiences can illustrate the most diverse types of challenges. The discussion is, nonetheless, also directly relevant to represented parties because many of the pre-court procedural steps and evidence preparation stages are completed without advocates or with minimal input from them (e.g. advocates do not attend interviews with social services – see Table 1). The Element also touches upon discursive practices in cases heard by magistrates (though magistrates are only involved in child-related proceedings with low safeguarding concerns as other family and civil cases are heard by professional judges) and situations in which expert witnesses are involved. Irrespective of the layperson's role, the differences in lay and legal communicative agendas and styles create tensions (cf. Heffer et al. 2013; Tkacukova 2016), which impacts the opportunities the lay person receives or the extent to which they actively seek such opportunities when engaging with the proceedings (Grieshofer 2022b).

The obvious barriers in legal–lay discourse are of linguistic nature and range from comprehension-related through conceptual or cognitive to communicative barriers. These cannot be easily addressed because of underlying conceptual complexity of legal texts, which often need to be formulated through complex lexical and syntactic constructions: the legal texts are written to ensure all-inclusiveness, accuracy and unambiguity of interpretation, but that necessarily reduces their clarity and transparency (Bhatia and Bhatia 2011; Gibbons 2003: 162–169; Stark 1994). The plain language movement has been successful in raising the public and law professionals' awareness of the importance of transparent communication and establishing guidelines for simplifying linguistic features, explaining terminology, expressing concepts more explicitly, and ensuring clear layout and organisational structure (Adler 2012). But full transparency is illusive: comprehension involves not only the understanding of individual concepts but also their inherent meaning, which can only be gained through the knowledge of procedure rules, legal doctrines and judicial decision-making principles (Assy 2011; Azuelos-Atias 2011). Even commonly used words, which have a distinct legal meaning, or short words (e.g. conjunctions) can be confusing for the layperson if they are unfamiliar with their use in the specialised legal discourse (Yeung and Leung 2019).

Comprehension-related challenges are experienced by participants in different institutional roles throughout different stages of legal proceedings. In criminal settings, for instance, the administration of justice and operation of the court system relies on jury members, who find the facts and apply the law to undisputed facts to return the verdict. The ability of the jury to fulfil their duty, however, depends on the clarity of jury instructions. Balancing the comprehensibility of jury instructions with the practicalities of litigation presents an ongoing challenge.

In the past, the comprehensibility of jury instructions was considerably reduced due to the fact that the instructions were delivered in the spoken mode but drew on the written legal discourse conventions, such as the use of long and complex sentences, inclusion of technical vocabulary and reliance on the concepts which are part of distinct legal cognitive schema ('beyond reasonable doubt'), without enabling jurors to engage with the text or request a clarification (Dumas 2002; Tiersma 2000). In recognition of comprehension-related difficulties experienced by jurors, the practice of delivering jury instructions in England and Wales has undergone several changes. The text written by the judge is now agreed on by the defence and prosecution and, importantly, the framing of the standard of proof 'beyond reasonable doubt' has been replaced with the single adjective 'sure' (cf. Heffer 2007). Yet, even the shift towards a seemingly comprehensible 'sure' to express the standard of proof is fraught with problems. The conceptual vagueness of the adjective 'sure' and its link to the common everyday use can result in very subjective interpretations of the standard of proof, as shown in *R v Mohammad* [2022] EWCA Crim 380, in which forensic linguists Heffer and Coulthard submitted evidence arguing for the unsatisfactory use of 'sure' as the standard of proof in the current practice of directing jury members. This is a prime example of the urgent need for linguistic expertise to be embedded in the discursive practices of legal professionals and court services. But the institutional habitus of delivering jury instructions resonates a performative ritual (Heffer 2013), which favours institutional authoritativeness and litigation certainty by following the established practice because taking a more communicative approach and enhancing the jury's comprehension may potentially lead to an appeal on the basis of mistrial.

Beyond comprehension-related difficulties, a further challenge for lay participants is to actively contribute to the interaction in legal settings and engage with spoken and written legal discourse. Discursive competence in a specialised domain, such as legal discourse, integrates different types of competences (Bhatia 2004: 144): textual competence (comprehension and production of written and spoken texts which follow the relevant genre requirements and stylistic characteristics) and generic and social competences (strategic use of language to participate in the professional domain and institutional context and achieve the results, despite the institutional structural and procedural restrictions). Discursive competence is acquired through training and experience; the interpretation and application of law to specific situations or construction of coherent legal arguments thus cannot be achieved, for instance, as a result of reading a plain language information booklet (Assy 2011). Even the litigants' level of education or degree of professional expertise in another area does not constitute decisive factors when it comes to their ability to fully engage with the proceedings (Trinder et al. 2014). For first-time court users, it is especially challenging to foresee how the proceedings develop and how their narratives need to be reinterpreted and recontextualised for different stages of the proceedings. It is mainly the experience with previous court proceedings that helps repeat court users acquire discursive skills and perform better in court (Grieshofer 2022b; Trinder et al. 2014). Even throughout the duration of long court cases which potentially present an opportunity to gain court experience, SRLs have been shown to only achieve a variable degree of improvement of their litigation skills (Tkacukova 2010).

Communicative issues in legal–lay discourse do not arise only because of deficiencies in the layperson's competencies in legal settings. A crucial part of the puzzle is the way communication is orchestrated throughout the legal proceedings, breaching many linguistic principles and everyday communication rules. For instance, the pinnacle of legal–lay interaction in adversarial settings, the witness examination phase, relies on manipulative questioning strategies which impose pre-determined turn-taking and types of turns and break many interaction rules common in everyday conversations: anyone in the witness box is limited to answering questions and thus have to follow the agenda and communicative goals of the examiner (Tkacukova 2010). The aim of cross-examination is to control the testimony by asking coercive closed questions which frame the events or facts in the way the cross-examiner wishes to and, through achieving this, to constrain the witness to minimal yes/no responses (Danet et al. 1980; Harris 1984; Heritage 2002; Philips 1987; Walker 1987; Woodbury 1984). Witness examination is the single occasion witnesses and litigants can provide their oral testimony in court. So it is particularly problematic that the discursive tools available to cross-examiners (e.g. control over topics and their sequence, formulation and evaluation of facts, and timing, content and interpretation of responses – see Thornborrow 2014; Tkacukova 2016) create an imbalance in power relations; even if the cross-examinee contests, corrects or denies the propositions implied in the questions (Janney 2002; Newbury and Johnson 2006), cross-examiners can typically regain control. It is becoming increasingly clear that cross-examination, as a way of eliciting and testing evidence, is problematic for vulnerable victims and witnesses as well as anyone who finds themselves in the witness box (Doak et al. 2021; Ellison 2001).

The discursive practices normalised in legal proceedings allow lay narratives to be controlled, reinterpreted and framed and reframed according to the practices and conventions of legal proceedings. The art of eliciting evidence is a crucial part of legal–lay interactions, but this aspect has so far been largely ignored in research and practice (cf. Grieshofer 2023b). When unsupported, the

SRLs' accounts can be overly emotional and seemingly unfocused (Trinder et al. 2014) or, at least, this is how they are perceived by professionals. Conley and O'Barr (1998, 1988) report that lay litigants tend to present relational and inductive accounts, which focus on the litigants' good character and good intentions, their personal life and social status, leaving the audience to make their own inferences as to agency, blame and responsibility (Conley and O'Barr 1998: 67–68; O'Barr and Conley 1985). The courts and judiciary, on the other hand, expect to be presented with rule-oriented and deductive narratives, which conform to the logic of law and its rules, structuring the accounts sequentially, identifying the parties and their relationships and explicitly stating their obligations and violations of law (Conley and O'Barr 1998; O'Barr and Conley 1985). Although it is easier to deal with the structure and content of rule-oriented accounts (Conley and O'Barr 1998: 68–74), what needs to be acknowledged is that evidential rules impose narrativisation strategies which are in discrepancy with lay narrativisation styles common in everyday interactions (O'Barr and Conley 1985). The existing evidence points to the fact that litigants whose accounts do not meet the criteria tend to have lower rates of court satisfaction and are less successful in their claims (O'Barr 1982), especially if they are not supported by the judiciary, lawyers or court staff (cf. Trinder et al. 2014; Gracean 2014).

As a result of all the aforementioned communicative and discursive barriers, it is common that victims feel re-victimised (cf. Matoesian 2001; Ehrlich 2010; Hunter et al. 2020), defendants feel they cannot escape being presented in the blame frame (cf. Baffy and Marsters 2015), litigants leave the court feeling they were not given an opportunity to share their side of the story (Grieshofer 2023b; Hunter et al. 2020), and even expert witnesses are not given an opportunity to expand on their testimony (Gray 2010; Hobbs 2003). Consequently, lay people experience attitudinal barriers as they become disengaged from the proceedings and lose trust in the system, especially if they are not given an opportunity to share their story the way they are comfortable with or if they do not feel their perspective is considered or even noted (Grieshofer 2022c; McKeever et al. 2018).

The further type of challenge highlighted in socio-legal literature is procedural barriers experienced by lay court users (Smith et al. 2017; Trinder et al. 2014). This is especially relevant for adversarial settings as an inherent part of adversarialism is its procedural complexity (Kessler 2004: section 1). It is procedural advice, rather than purely legal advice on substantive law, that has most potential to help lay court users move their cases forward (cf. Sandefur 2015; Williams 2011). The Element argues that court procedures impact elicitation and narrativisation strategies and thus define when and how court users can present their narratives. By establishing the link between procedural and discursive aspects of county and family court proceedings, the theoretical framework presented here contributes to the development of discursive strategies for enhancing legal–lay communication as part of procedural changes and court reforms.

3 Discourse of Civil and Family Proceedings

Research on language use in courtroom and legal settings traditionally falls under the broader remit of forensic linguistics and tends to be grouped into two research areas: legal discourse and courtroom discourse (Cotterill 2002; Coulthard et al. 2021; Gibbons 2014, 2003; Heffer et al. 2013; Tiersma and Solan 2012). While studies in legal discourse focus on the analysis of written legal texts and explore their linguistic complexity and interpretation methods (e.g. Tiersma and Solan 2012; Tiersma 1999; Solan 2019; Adler 2012), courtroom discourse studies focus on spoken interactions during court proceedings and reflect on inequalities in power relations during legal–lay interactions, narrativisation strategies, witness examination strategies, legal rhetoric (e.g. Cotterill 2003; Heffer 2005; Stygall 2012; Bednarek 2014). The separation of the two areas is guided by the type of data explored and the corresponding methodological approaches used, but it is also driven by the fact that most of the existing research on courtroom discourse has focused on criminal trials (e.g. Cotterill 2003; Heffer 2005; Bednarek 2014; Coulthard et al. 2021), with only a few studies focusing on non-criminal proceedings (Lowndes 2007; Tkacukova 2010, 2015).

The Element argues that it is important to breach the disciplinary boundaries by introducing a more unified concept of the 'discourse of legal proceedings', which includes pre-court stages and court hearings (Grieshofer 2022b) and highlights the continuity between the predominantly written texts which shape the evidentiary stages (e.g. legislation, practice directions, court forms, reports, witness statements) and the interactive stages during court hearings (cf. Haworth 2013; Komter 2013; Johnson 2013). The term, the discourse of legal proceedings, helps reflect on the discursive journey of court users while also highlighting the link between different types of discourses and court processes and procedures embedded in legal proceedings. As a result, it connects socio-legal research interests to diverse communicative aspects across the proceedings and clarifies the relevance of linguistic input to socio-legal studies (cf. Grieshofer 2023b; Tkacukova 2020, 2016).

The other advantage of the term introduced here lies in its prospect to encourage researchers to specify the type of proceedings (e.g. the discourse of criminal proceedings, the discourse of small claims). Given that most research has so far focused on criminal cases, criminal settings have defined what we know about courtroom discourse. Yet, there are crucial differences between criminal and non-criminal proceedings in, for instance, the type of courts and physical arrangements within courtrooms: the family and county hearings tend to be held in smaller courtrooms and the layout of many of the hearing rooms resembles standard meeting rooms. Similarly, the rhetoric of legal parties is directed towards the judiciary as the primary addressees, whereas the audience design in criminal proceedings is much more complex as the testimony is reoriented from police interviews to addressing the jury and judiciary in court-room settings (cf. Haworth 2013). There are two further crucial differences between criminal and non-criminal proceedings, which particularly impact the discursive practices of civil and family proceedings throughout all their stages. From the legal-discursive perspective, the first difference is the standard of the burden of proof (i.e. 'on the balance of probabilities' in civil and family proceedings vs. 'beyond reasonable doubt' in criminal proceedings), which, as a result, translates into crucial distinctions in evidence threshold and proced-ure rules and legislation regulating evidence gathering and submission (Kaplow 2011; Cheng and Nunn 2019). For instance, the interviews with families conducted by social workers are not audio-recorded and interviewers simply summarise the responses in their reports, whereas police interviews are recorded and transcribed verbatim. As a result of a lower standard of evidence threshold in family proceedings, there is no traceable evidence of the original conversations between social workers and parents/children (see Section 5 for a more detailed discussion on language data management).

The other crucial difference between criminal and non-criminal proceedings lies in the role of the layperson. In criminal cases, it is mainly the police and lawyers who identify the legal issues, collect evidence and initiate the proceed-ings; the layperson (victim, defendant, witness) is thus limited to assisting the investigations by being interviewed and interacting with the law enforcement agencies. Court users in civil and family proceedings, however, have to engage with the proceedings and the evidence gathering stage more actively, irrespect-ive of whether they are represented by a lawyer or not (e.g. bank statements tend to be provided by the parties, witness statements are written by the parties). They also need to engage with court forms, legal information, written legal documents and genres which would traditionally be considered as part of written legal discourse (see Tables 1 and 2). The legal–lay communication challenges thus extend to pre-court and court stages and should be considered as part of all procedural stages rather than just court discourse (Grieshofer 2023b).

Even within non-criminal settings, there is a lot of variety between cases heard across different types of courts and tribunals: civil cases, public family cases, private family cases and a wide range of tribunal proceedings. Each of these types of proceedings is unique in the level of formality, legal representation pattern, procedural and evidential rules, and the resulting discursive practices (McKeever 2020; Grieshofer 2022b). For instance, there are crucial discursive differences guided by procedural differences even within private family proceedings; private family cases include divorce proceedings, child arrangements proceedings and financial remedy proceedings, each with slightly different discursive characteristics (e.g. child arrangements proceedings are arguably less technical and mainly draw on the child welfare principle, whereas the financial remedy proceedings cover many financial and legal concepts). These differences feed into diverse procedural and discursive challenges and need to be accounted for as part of legal–lay discursive practices.

But there is also a crucial similarity across different types of criminal and non-criminal proceedings, given by the fact that narrativisation plays a key role in legal contexts, as has been illustrated in the existing research on courtroom discourse in criminal settings (e.g. Cotterill 2003; Harris 2005, 2001; Heffer 2005; Matoesian 2001). Although narrativisation in legal settings is different from narrativisation in everyday discourse, it is the framing of narratives and their development throughout the proceedings that defines the relevance and strength of the parties' cases (Conley and O'Barr 1990; O'Barr and Conley 1991; Tkacukova 2016). In adversarialism, narratives are shared and constantly (re)framed and (re)interpreted as part of the goal-oriented and persuasive character of trials (Cotterill 2003: 24). In criminal settings, narrativisation is a complex and multi-perspectival process (Cotterill 2003: 25), which involves master narratives of monologic nature with fictional elements (opening and closing speeches) and satellite narratives which contribute to master narratives but are more factual as they are created during witness examination (Gibbons 2003: 155; Coulthard and Johnson 2007: 99; Harris 2005: 218–224). Narrative construction is thus accompanied by narrative disjunction (Coulthard and Johnson 2007: 111). The fragmentation of satellite narratives is unavoidable due to multiple factors: the question/answer pattern of interaction follows the examiner's agenda; the original evidence is constantly reinterpreted (especially during different witness examination stages); the order of witnesses is driven by practicalities and legal coherence rather than narrative coherence (Harris 2005: 216); the evidence is collected from witnesses on several occasions and then presented in different formats for different communicative purposes and multiple asynchronous audiences (Haworth 2013).

The same narrativisation features apply to non-criminal proceedings, but what makes narrativisation even more complex for court users in family and civil settings is that the parties need to perform a more active role in defining the legal issues and evidencing them. Even just the first step of identifying a problem as a legal issue has been shown as a challenge for the layperson: circumstances which can be resolved by taking legal action often go unnoticed if legal advice is not available (Genn 1999). Similarly, once the court user is ready to take legal action, the first step of starting the proceedings involves completing court forms which are linguistically complex and, as a genre for evidence elicitation, often present one of the first discursive challenges for court users' narrativisation (Grieshofer 2023a; Grieshofer et al. 2021).

Furthermore, narrativisation in family and county courts is affected by the judicial variability as judges often change in between hearings and there is no guarantee that the final hearing would be heard by the same judge as any of the previous hearings (though, in theory, many small claims cases only require one hearing if all the evidentiary stages are completed prior to the court appearance). This is especially the case in private family proceedings which tend to be presided by different judges, and the parties thus have to repeat their stories throughout different hearings. The variability in the judicial style also impacts the parties' opportunities to engage as judges vary in, for instance, the extent to which they explain matters, the extent to which their explanations are comprehensible, how they elicit information, whether they lean towards a more adversarial or inquisitorial approach to case management (cf. Hunter 2005; Hunter et al. 2008; Hunter et al. 2016; Trinder et al. 2014; Conley and O'Barr 1988, 1990: chapter 5; Tkacukova 2015).

Such narrativisation complexities are compounded in protracted proceedings as there is more scope for changing the context of narrative evolution (Cotterill 2002: 149). For instance, child-related proceedings tend to last for approximately a year or even longer (*Court Statistics for England and Wales* 2023), and as children grow up and family circumstances change, the initial narratives require amendments. Equally, the trial story (Heffer 2005: 69) is also evolving constantly as at each hearing new procedural decisions are taken, which impacts the scope of the parties' narratives (see Section 6).

Finally, narrativisation in family and county court settings is particularly susceptible to the changes in the overall institutional narrative, which is influenced by political and socio-economic changes and developments in the legal professional services landscape. The withdrawal of large pockets of legal aid post-LASPO has created the conditions in which courts struggle to meet SRLs' needs. As LASPO particularly diminished legal aid available for private family disputes, the political solution was to make mediation in private family

proceedings compulsory and to reinforce out-of-court dispute resolution opportunities. There are, however, serious concerns among legal practitioners about
the context in which mediations and out-of-court negotiations happen and the
lack of support for vulnerable parties (Maclean and Eekelaar 2016).
Nevertheless, the parties are urged to settle at different points and the presump-
tion is that they will do so (Maclean 2010; Trinder et al. 2014). For instance,
child-related proceedings or financial remedy proceedings cannot start unless
there is evidence that the parties attempted mediation or that parties are exempt
from mediation (e.g. due to domestic violence allegations). Moreover, during
and after each hearing, the parties are encouraged by the judiciary to negotiate
and settle the case (unless there are serious safeguarding concerns in the child-
related proceedings). As a result, many of the private family cases do not
proceed to the final hearing, which leads to several limitations: the proceedings
do not reach the stage of full disclosure or the stage of the judiciary's input into
possible outcomes (Maclean 2010); the narratives shared during pre-court
stages become more important than court narrativisation stages (Grieshofer
2022b); the out-of-court landscape of legal proceedings remains largely unex-
plored from the point of view of institutional statistics or scholarly research. It is
thus important to retain the awareness of the discursive continuity of the
proceedings and to identify communicative aims at each stage in order to
understand diverse barriers and limitations within the discursive context of
legal proceedings.

4 Discursive Practices, Procedural Justice and Legal Participation

Given the continuous role of language and communication throughout the
different stages of legal processes and procedures (Grieshofer 2022b) and the
textual travels of evidence handover between statutory agencies (Heffer et al.
2013), it is crucial to establish discursive practices as a key aspect to be
considered in research and practice. Discursive practices combine text-
internal and text-external aspects embedded within institutional practices
(pertinent to courts and the justice system) and professional practices (followed
by the judiciary, advocates and court staff – cf. Bhatia 2006). This essentially
means that exploring discursive practices incorporates exploring how spoken or
written texts and interactions are produced and interpreted within the boundaries of professional conventions as well as institutional cultures influenced by
socio-political changes (Bhatia 2006, 2004). In the context of lower courts, the
post-LASPO influx of SRLs has had a detrimental impact on institutional and
professional practices. The moment a party is self-represented, the role of
everyone involved in legal proceedings changes: the judiciary need to provide

more explanation, opposing lawyers need to take more responsibility for drafting court orders and preparing court bundles, court staff need to support court users with administrative steps (Tkacukova 2015; Trinder et al. 2014). Further, the SRLs' role is ambiguous as they do not have the same interactional space as advocates would normally have: SRLs are limited in conducting cross-examination (e.g. SRLs are asked to prepare a list of cross-examination questions which are then read out by the judiciary), presenting their case (e.g. the judiciary tend to ask the represented party to present the case first even if they represent a respondent and should in theory follow the applicant's overview) or instructing an expert witness (e.g. SRLs experience practical barriers when trying to find and instruct an expert witness – cf. Trinder et al. 2014; Tkacukova 2016; Moorhead 2007). As a result, on the one hand, SRLs cannot be expected to possess discursive competence to represent themselves effectively (Grieshofer 2023b) and, on the other hand, the legal system is not designed to meet SRLs' needs (Mant 2022).

In this stalemate position, it is attention to discursive practices that has the potential to enhance the legal–lay interface of court processes and procedures (Grieshofer 2023b). From the practical perspective, it is useful to highlight the reciprocal nature of discursive practices as they include elicitation and narrativisation practices and these are implemented on the interpersonal level during court interactions and institutional level during pre-court and court stages. The elicitation and narrativisation on the institutional level involves such complex genres as court forms, witness statements, evidence provision, court bundles, pre-court investigations conducted by statutory agencies (e.g. social services). The institutional discursive practices are pre-defined by procedure rules and practice directions which determine how cases are managed, when the evidence is collected and what decision can be taken at which stage (cf. *CPR Rules and Directions*). On the interpersonal level, the genres and other communicative elements are less defined, but court processes and procedures leave little room for adjustments as each hearing has a specific communicative goal and the judiciary's role is limited to case management in accordance with individual procedural stages (cf. Moorhead 2007; Ainsworth 2015, see also Tables 1 and 2). Given the procedural and discursive complexities court users have to navigate, the minimum support the legal system is supposed to provide is access to information. Information provision practices are an integral part of elicitation and narrativisation practices. Yet, court forms, court communication and legal and procedural information are notoriously difficult to engage with (Grieshofer 2022c). This complicates elicitation and narrativisation strategies during pre-court stages if court users cannot understand what is required, and during court hearings if court users fail to complete the pre-court stages (cf. Grieshofer et al. 2021; Grieshofer 2023a).

Discursive practices are an inherent part of court processes and procedures throughout the whole duration of legal proceedings.

In fact, discursive practices are at the heart of how court users experience and evaluate justice. The extensive body of literature on procedural justice (Thibaut and Walker 1975) shows that people are interested in not only the outcomes of their claims but also how their disputes are processed: citizens are more likely to accept outcomes, including unfavourable outcomes, if they feel the decisions were reached following fair decision-making processes and they were treated fairly and had an opportunity to express their side of the story (MacCoun 2005; Tyler 2000). The significance of individuals' perceptions of fairness lies in the fact that such perceptions encourage the public to comply with the law (Lind et al. 1990) and, in the immediate context, encourage court users to engage with courts. To break down the concept, Sela (2018) summarises four dimensions which support access to procedural justice:

- process control (control over the opportunity to present evidence);
- decision control (control over the final outcome);
- interactional justice (the decision-maker's treatment of a person with politeness, dignity and respect);
- and informational justice (the availability of information and explanations about the process and its justification)

(Sela 2018: 106).

All of the components rely on efficient written and spoken communication in interactive and asynchronous formats during court and out-of-court stages of the proceedings. Three of the components are directly dependent on discursive practices on the institutional and interpersonal levels: *process control* and *interactional justice* rely on elicitation and narrativisation practices and interaction management; *informational justice* relies on comprehensibility and transparency of information provision. *Decision control* is indirectly dependent on the provision of transparent procedural information and elicitation and narrativisation practices: limited legal and procedural understanding can prevent court users from foreseeing different exit options, restrict them in negotiation strategies or even stop them from trying to negotiate (cf. Trinder et al. 2014; Smith et al. 2017).

When it comes to court users accessing the tenets of procedural justice, *decision control* is restricted by the fact that institutions generally reserve the right to limit the scope of viable outcomes and, in legal settings, the justice system can only offer a limited number of options (MacCoun 2005). Similarly, the predefined nature of court processes and procedures diminishes the court users' opportunity to have any impact on *process control* and even minimises the judiciary's input in case management, procedural steps or how and when the evidence can be presented (Grieshofer 2023b; Hunter et al. 2020). *Informational justice* is equally not easy to achieve, but other tenets of procedural justice rely on it. There are different types of information court users need to access: legal, procedural, administrative. Unfortunately, court users find it difficult to find the relevant information online or in court guidance documents due to multiple limitations: generic nature of the information, lack of clear cross-referencing to relevant legislation, complex language, exclusion of explanations relevant for SRLs, biased or misleading content (Grieshofer et al. 2021; Grieshofer 2023a & 2022c). The HM Courts and Tribunals Service's (HMCTS) slow pace with addressing the issues pertinent to informational justice complicates court users' access to procedural justice (Grieshofer et al. 2021). Deficiencies in information provision on the institutional level essentially create conditions for the exclusion of unrepresented court users from participating efficiently in the discourse of legal proceedings and result in discursive discrimination (cf. Boréus 2006).

Interactional justice is the only aspect of procedural justice where there is some potential to meet court users' needs during court hearings (the pre-court stages of interactional justice are still defined by rigid court processes and procedures). To add to Sela's definition of interactional justice, the experience of court users will largely depend on the extent to which they are allowed to express their voice and contribute to the hearings and the proceedings (cf. Tyler 2000; MacCoun 2005; McKeever 2020; Grieshofer 2022b). This is also the key factor which contributes to the effective legal participation (Jacobson 2020), though the socio-legal discussions of legal participation principles tend to be limited to the physical provision of special measures in cases involving vulnerable participants (e.g. legal professionals not wearing wigs or gowns, vulnerable participants appearing behind screens or via video link). The discursive aspects apply to any trial participant (represented, unrepresented, vulnerable court users or witnesses) and gain significance when exploring effective legal participation during hearings and out-of-court stages (Grieshofer 2023b). In linguistic terms, the court users' degree of participation depends on the interactive space they are given, the interactive tools they can access (e.g. if they can start new topics or if they are limited to responding to questions) and their discursive competence. In practice, the extent to which courts and tribunals accommodate individual needs of lay people involved in the proceedings depends on practice directions, procedure rules, appellate decisions and professional discursive practices (Hunter 2020), which differ across different types of legal proceedings and adjudicative approaches (cf. McKeever 2020).

The systemic design of adversarialism poses a paradox in relation to interactional justice, legal participation and, more generally, court users' opportunities to express their voices. According to Ainsworth (2015), adversarial systems are more supportive of procedural justice tenets because they are built on the principle that court users (and their lawyers as proxies) construct and control the narratives. But in lower courts, this advantage is outweighed by the fact that many litigants have to resort to self-representation, despite often having very limited knowledge of relevant law or procedures. The procedural complexities embedded in adversarialism and the passive role of the judiciary in establishing the facts of the case limit interactional justice and process control during pre-court and court stages of the proceedings. Though during court hearings, the attitudes and approaches of individual judges and advocates play a defining role in how trial participants are treated and supported in their active and effective participation (Hunter 2020). The hearings in which the judiciary move away from adversarialism and adopt elements of inquisitorial approach were found to be generally beneficial for SRLs as such support (e.g. tailored elicitation of evidence and narratives) allowed them to present their arguments and move their cases forward (Trinder et al. 2014). But if elicitation practices adopted are not accommodating enough, interactional justice is complicated by the (previously discussed) dichotomy between the lay narrativisation strategies and the requirements on legal narrativisation set by courts and the legal profession. Correspondingly, litigants presenting relational accounts, as opposed to fulfilling the expectation for rule-based accounts, are less successful in their cases and are more likely to be dissatisfied with the process (O'Barr and Conley 1991).

The long-standing criticism of the adversarial approach points to deficiencies in discursive practices, interactional justice and process control: the absolute control lawyers have over the testimony of the witnesses (Ainsworth 2015); strong focus on the contesting narratives creating an unnecessarily antagonistic environment; parties' narratives emphasising their interests rather than an effective resolution of the problem; priority given to evidencing the narrative rather than truth seeking; inequality between parties due to the unaffordability of legal support; imbalance between the parties' responsibilities due to the systemic implications of the doctrine of the burden of proof; procedural complexity (Ainsworth 2015; Block and Parker 2004; Freiberg 2011; Firestone and Weinstein 2004; King et al. 2014; Lande 2003; McIntosh et al. 2008; Moorhead 2007). This has led many adversarial jurisdictions to start considering different alternative models, such as enabling, problem-solving, investigative, restorative, therapeutic, collaborative, participatory approaches (e.g. King et al. 2014; Thomas 2012; Hunter et al. 2020), but these procedures tend to be limited to specific pilots or individual types of proceedings (e.g. juvenile drug courts – *Problem-solving Courts* 2019). Nevertheless, the motivation behind the change is often driven by the realisation that institutional and interpersonal communication does not work for court users and the system needs to reorient towards a more user-friendly and problem-solving approach (cf. Hunter et al. 2020).

In sum, court processes, procedure rules and practice directions define the discursive practices throughout all the stages of legal proceedings; the discursive practices, in turn, impact legal–lay communication and court users' access to procedural justice. Problem-solving courts can serve as a useful example here: they aim to retain an open-enquiry approach during regular hearings with the same judge and meetings with the support team in out-of-court settings, which contributes to the success of this type of community courts in reducing reoffence rates (*Problem-solving Courts* 2019). This demonstrates that the system redesign can start with the exploration of discursive practices, or at least employ an iterative approach to adjusting the discursive and procedural aspects simultaneously. The link between discursive practices, procedural justice and efficient legal participation should undoubtedly be part of systemic reforms and procedural changes as well as an established area of improvement for professional legal education and training purposes (cf. Moorhead 2007).

5 Language Data and Empirical Methods

Legal settings abound with language data and linguistics offers the methodological tools for exploring many critical research avenues with respect to: how law is constructed, performed and interpreted through the analysis of written and spoken texts and interactions, how trial participants engage with the legal system, how legal procedures position the participants of legal proceedings or how courts assess the participants' performances (Luchjenbroers and Aldridge 2008). Yet, most of language data for linguistic research in legal contexts can be difficult to access: it is either not collected at all by court services or collected but not made available for research purposes (or even to parties themselves).

For instance, most court proceedings in England and Wales are audio-recorded, but according to the current HMCTS data access policies, the recordings of court hearings are not released to researchers or the parties. It is only trial transcripts made by a court assigned transcriber that can be made available to the parties or, potentially, researchers. But the transcription services are very costly and the usability of trial transcripts for linguistic research is flawed with limitations since the transcription process inadvertently introduces multiple changes to the original interactions: such meaning-bearing suprasegmental features as intonation or pauses often disappear; contextual references become decontextualised; placing of punctuation can change the meaning of original utterances; any form of misunderstanding or lack of awareness leads to inaccuracies; and there are multiple inconsistencies across individual transcription practices (Eades 1996; Fraser 2003; Haworth 2013, 2018; Richardson et al. 2022; Walker 1986, 1990). But there are also contexts which are even more challenging from the perspective of data collection and institutional language data management, such as procedural stages during which interactions are not even recorded. For instance, immigration tribunal hearings tend to rely on the notes of case workers and panel members and thus do not have a traceable or transparent record of original interactions or the evidence elicited during the proceedings (Gibb 2019; Grieshofer 2022a).

There is little doubt that a more rigorous process of collecting, managing and sharing language data for research and evidentiary purposes needs to be established. The transparency and fairness of the justice system depends on the quality of data collection processes, including the type and format of data collected (cf. Jay et al. 2020; Grieshofer 2022b). Managing language data in accordance with fundamental linguistic principles (e.g. ensuring that audio recordings are played in court instead of transcripts being read out) will help courts meet the rules of physical evidence preservation (Haworth 2018). Moreover, collecting and releasing language data for research purposes will enable researchers to analyse case-level data and ultimately enhance access to procedural justice. Above all, the current status quo in relation to the management of language data is unacceptable and a higher benchmark for ensuring the quality assurance measures for language data management need to urgently become part of institutional and professional ethos.

As the situation stands, linguists tend to limit themselves to investigating the settings in which the data is available and thus explore interactions from legal proceedings by accessing court transcripts (e.g. transcripts prepared for appeals can sometimes be acquired for free) or public releases of transcripts or recordings from prominent cases (e.g. Tkacukova 2015, 2010; Cotterill 2003; Heffer 2005; Bednarek 2014) or, alternatively, focus on small case studies from private interactions (e.g. Reynolds 2020). This type of data is instrumental for analysing specific aspects of legal–lay interactions in legal settings but cannot always reflect on the discourse of the routine cases, which are tried in lower courts on a daily basis and are relevant for the majority of court users. To examine everyday court cases, socio-legal scholars tend to rely on court observations in combination with interviews and other empirical methods: many influential research studies have drawn on field work and court observations in particular to identify challenges in family proceedings and small claims cases (e.g. Trinder et al. 2014; Smith et al. 2017; Moorhead and Sefton 2005). Combining theory with practice, socio-legal ethnography is suitable for the examination of broader issues within the legal system or even the exploration of wider global trends, despite potential reservations about generalisations that could be made based on field work (Flood 2005).

One challenge for linguists is that observations are difficult to capture, especially since it is only possible to make notes and, irrespective of how detailed the notes are or whether there is an attempt to create a verbatim transcript using a shorthand method, any written record will only be partial and suffer from similar limitations as court transcripts. The solution used for this research study was to draw on a well-structured observation sheet with pre-defined (but also constantly evolving) measurable and clearly discernible features, thus creating notes through the instantaneous analysis contextualised during observations. The approach used for the study drew on the ethnography of communication as the main methodological framework, which puts emphasis on exploring communication in real-life situations as part of the socio-cultural context (Hymes 1962), thus aligning well with the investigation of court users' discursive competencies and identification of discursive practices embedded in court processes and procedures.

There are several further advantages this approach offers. Firstly, similarly to other ethnographically driven research, the ethnographic approach adopted here allows to combine relevant linguistic theories with discursive practices used in different stages of legal proceedings (cf. Hymes 1962; Carbaugh 1989). Secondly, ethnographic methods provide an opportunity to collect data in a naturalistic and realistic environment and explore interactions as they unfold turn-by-turn with the researcher being part of the inside and outside world (Carbaugh 1989; Flood 2005). Thirdly, the ethnography of communication specifically provides a framework for a detailed analysis of linguistic and social aspects of interactions based on the participants' linguistic behaviours and attitudes (Ejimabo 2015; Grieshofer 2022b; Sangasubana 2011). Finally and perhaps most importantly, the ethnography of communication lends itself well for documenting measurable features (e.g. interactional patterns or turn-taking management) and thus identifying recurring patterns across diverse settings or participant dynamics (Grieshofer 2022b). The additional benefit of conducting court observations is that fieldwork allows to explore real-life interactions as part of a sample of representative everyday cases, relate communicative strategies to extra-linguistic circumstances and the outcomes of hearings and swiftly reflect on topical systemic challenges without losing sight of the detail typical of qualitative research.

To ensure the data collection captured a representative and detailed overview of the communicative events observed, it was important to design an observation sheet that can cover all key discursive practices and can be used for interdisciplinary research needs (see Appendix). The observation sheet thus places the analytical focus on observable and measurable features and offers an opportunity to contextualise observations and reflections. Following the observation sheet, the notes identify and reflect the types of cases and hearings, participants and their roles, prevailing interaction patterns, turn-taking management, topics discussed and who they are introduced by, framing of topics by the parties, the role of the judiciary, source and type of explanations provided and the structure of the hearing. To capture the framing of topics discussed, it was important to transcribe verbatim whenever possible (if related to non-confidential information and it was physically possible to transcribe verbatim) or otherwise make detailed notes.

To complement court observations, the research also drew on interviews, survey, quantitative and qualitative analysis of court forms, and adopted the genre analysis approach to exploring discursive implications of Civil Procedure Rules (CPR) and Family Procedure Rules (FPR). Overall, the research is based on forty court observations (twenty-five child arrangements proceedings, five financial remedy proceedings and ten small claims cases), seventy-one questionnaires, fifty-one interviews with SRLs, twenty interviews with lawyers, thirty-five most frequently downloaded court forms from the HMCTS website and fifty court forms related to child arrangements as part of private and public family law proceedings. The mixed methods approach allowed the study to reflect on: lived court experiences of court users, in-court and out-of-court communication, narrativisation and elicitation practices on institutional and personal levels, systemic communication-related challenges, procedural barriers, discursive practices embedded in practice directions and procedure rules. Although the analysis of court observations draws on the themes discovered across all the research components, the Element mainly focuses on court observations, partially due to space limitations, but mainly due to the fact that ethnographic methods are currently under-represented in linguistic court research and should be more utilised (cf. D'hondt 2021).

It is also important to note that the original focus of the research study was on SRLs as self-representation is common in lower courts and SRLs' experiences showcase the diversity of legal–lay interaction challenges. Despite the original focus, the mixed methods approach enabled the study to draw conclusions in relation to systemic barriers to justice and thus reflect on not only the challenges experienced by SRLs but also represented clients. Investigating family and small claims courts from the position of court users who find themselves in the most discursively challenging circumstances (SRLs) enabled the study to test the systemic and procedural aspects and discover, for instance, why even represented clients may feel like they have no voice in the proceedings (cf. Hunter et al. 2020).

Given the significance of the layperson's role in collecting and compiling evidence in civil and family proceedings (see Section 3), all court users, irrespective of their legal representation status, experience some communicative and procedural barriers throughout pre-court and court stages (cf. Hunter et al. 2020). Further, the SRL status is not necessarily a uniform position as many decide to engage a lawyer in some capacity or for some hearings and therefore the legal representation pattern of many court proceedings varies in between the hearings (cf. Trinder et al. 2014).

The methodologically innovative framework presented here advances the field of courtroom discourse by establishing the communicative continuity within the discourse of legal proceedings and foregrounding discursive practices as part of procedural justice tenets and effective legal participation scaffolding. The research gains on importance at the time when the current legal system is not designed to meet the needs of diverse users, including SRLs, victims of domestic violence or children, and the justice system is looking for solutions through procedural changes, reforms and trialling of different approaches (cf. Hunter et al. 2020; King et al. 2014; Thomas 2012). It is institutional, court-level and case-level discursive practices that can help explain many of the current challenges, improve elicitation and narrativisation processes, contribute to procedural changes and court reforms and inspire further applied research.

6 Discursive Practices in Child Arrangement Proceedings

The aim of child arrangements proceedings is to determine who (usually which parent) the child or children will live with and who they will have contact with and when. The widespread concern shared among legal practitioners and researchers is that child arrangements proceedings mute the voices of children and their caregivers/parents, revictimise and retraumatise the victims of domestic violence, put children in danger by promoting parental contact at all costs, and process cases in an adversarial manner (Hunter et al. 2020). Vulnerable parents and children were found to feel that they were not heard or not supported as, despite the fact that the welfare principle (the principle of the best interests of the child) is of paramount importance in child-related proceedings, the adversarial approach shifts the focus towards the conflict between the parents, pushing them to contest their narratives rather than encouraging a problem-solving or trauma-aware approach (*Children's Experience of Private Family Proceedings* 2021; Firestone and Weinstein 2004; Hunter et al. 2020; McIntosh et al. 2008). It is important to note that incorporating children's opinions is not straightforward due to a number of complicating factors: social services only have very limited time allocated to interviewing children; eliciting children's views requires relevant experience and training; courts put limited weight on children's input (Grieshofer 2023b; Hunter et al. 2020: chapter 6). To address these challenges, different proposals for systemic changes keep emerging (cf. Hunter et al. 2020, *Children's Experience of Private Family Proceedings* 2021, Thomas 2012), but until now there has not been sufficient attention paid to the alignment between discursive practices and FPR (Grieshofer 2023b). The barriers to procedural justice thus persevere and any changes introduced so far have been very fragmentary (cf. *Improving Access to Justice for Separating Families* 2022).

To identify the communicative issues with the current proceedings, the framework presented in Table 1 (adapted from Grieshofer 2022b) provides an overview of discursive practices by detailing types and modes of elicitation and narrativisation genres, textual transformations, micro/macro narratives and communicative events and communicative aims of individual hearings. The overview presented in the form of the table builds on the practice directions embedded in the FPR, specifically 'Practice Direction 12b – Child Arrangements Programme'. This is an outline of what child arrangements proceedings entail; the actual proceedings are often more complex and may include more expert witnesses (e.g. psychologists) or more interim hearings. Sometimes additional interim hearings need to be added if, for instance, some of the pre-hearing requirements are not met in time. Nevertheless, as an approximation of the actual proceedings, Table 1 is sufficient to introduce an overview of elicitation and narrativisation practices (Cafcass stands for Children and Family Court Advisory and Support Service, the main statutory body and an independent service advising courts on the safety and well-being of children). With respect to the categorisation, the table encapsulates communicative aspects relevant to individual pre-hearing and hearing stages and categorises them according to the type and aim of genres (procedural, adversarial and adjudicative – see Gibbons 2003; Heffer 2013) and the source of narrative presentation (direct, lawyer-mediated, judge-mediated, expert-led and expert-framed – see Grieshofer 2022b).

What stands out is that narrativisation and elicitation practices in child arrangements proceedings are characterised by the following features: (1) a wide range of unfamiliar written genres which court users need to prepare during pre-court stages; (2) the prominence of pre-court narratives as opposed to court narrativisation opportunities; (3) the prevalence of procedural and adversarial genres as opposed to direct narratives; (4) high frequency of expert-led and expert-framed genres during pre-court stages; (5) the occurrence of adjudicative genres even before the hearings; (6) high occurrence of lawyer-mediated, lawyer-framed and judge-mediated narratives as opposed to direct

Table 1 Narrativisation in child arrangements cases (according to 'Practice Direction 12b – Child Arrangements Programme').

Narrativisation boundaries	Pre-hearing stages		Court hearings	
	Narrative genres	Narration	Narrative genres	Narration
	Communicative goal: initiating proceedings		**First Hearing Dispute Resolution Appointment (FHDRA)** **Communicative goal: case management, identifying issues**	
	Court forms (procedural, adversarial)	Direct (parties or lawyer)	Out-of-court negotiations	Direct (parties) or lawyer-mediated
	Risk identification interview with a Children and Family Court Advisory and Support Service (Cafcass) worker (procedural, adversarial)	Expert-led (Cafcass worker, parties)	Presenting the case/position (adversarial)	Direct (parties) or lawyer-framed
	Cafcass safeguarding report (procedural, adjudicative)	Expert-framed (Cafcass)	Case management and narrowing down issues (procedural, adversarial, adjudicative)	Judge-mediated (judge and parties or their lawyers)
			Directions, interim court order or consent order (procedural, adjudicative)	Directive for narrative scope (judiciary)
	Communicative goal: preparing evidence		**Directions/Dispute Resolution Appointment (DRA)** **Communicative goal: case management, narrowing down issues**	
	Interviews for the section 7 Cafcass report (procedural, adversarial)	Expert-led (Cafcass worker, parties)	Out-of-court negotiations	Direct (parties) or lawyer-mediated
	Cafcass section 7 report (procedural, adjudicative elements)	Expert-framed (Cafcass)	Presenting the case/position (adversarial)	Direct (parties) or lawyer-framed
			Case management and narrowing down issues (procedural, adversarial, adjudicative)	Judge-mediated (judge and parties or their lawyers)
			Directions, interim court order or consent order (procedural, adjudicative)	Directive for narrative scope (judge)
	Communicative goal: preparing further evidence		**Fact finding hearing/Interim hearings (in case of domestic violence allegations)** **Communicative goal: consider the evidence around domestic abuse allegations**	
	Further evidence, statement of facts/issues, witness statements/skeleton arguments (procedural, adversarial)	Direct, antagonistic (applicant, then respondent)	Presenting the case/position (adversarial)	Direct (parties) or lawyer-framed
	Scott Schedule, i.e. numbered list of allegations and responses to these (adversarial)	Direct, antagonistic (applicant, then respondent)	Case management and narrowing down issues (procedural, adversarial, adjudicative)	Judge-mediated (judge and parties or their lawyers)
	Court bundle (procedural, adversarial)	All narrations	Witness examination (adversarial)	Direct and lawyer-framed (parties, lawyers, judiciary)
			Decision as to allegations (adjudicative, procedural)	Directive for narrative scope (judge)
	Communicative goal: finalising court bundle		**Final hearing** **Communicative goal: consider all evidence and make the final decision**	
	Court bundle (procedural, adversarial)	Direct, expert-framed	Presenting the case/position (adversarial)	Direct (parties) or lawyer-framed
			Case management and narrowing down issues (procedural, adversarial, adjudicative)	Judge-mediated (judge and parties or their lawyers)
			Witness examination (adversarial)	Direct and lawyer-framed (parties, lawyers, judge)
			Child Arrangements Order (adjudicative)	Directive for post-proceedings stage (judge)

Evidential stages — Submissions

Court procedures (CPR/FPR), legal framework, discursive practices, justice system narrative narratives from parties; (7) gradual narrowing of the narrativisation scope after each hearing; (8) the prevalence of procedural focus in the initial hearings (cf. Grieshofer 2022b, 2023b). As a result, the parties can only relate their family situation through fragmented narratives which are elicited and shared through different means and by different professionals.

All of this is in stark contrast to information elicitation models which adhere to the principles of communication management and follow an open-enquiry elicitation approach; for instance, the UK model of police interviews is recognised as the ethical model of evidence elicitation (cf. Grant 2010): it starts with eliciting a free narrative account in response to open-ended questions before restricting the interviewee to responding to closed questions which challenge their accounts; the final stage is then reserved for summarising the account elicited to ensure the interviewee and interviewer arrive at a consolidated version (cf. MacLeod and Haworth 2017). By comparison, the first pre-court stage in child arrangements proceedings requires court users to summarise their cases in response to questions in court forms and questions asked by a Cafcass officer over the phone. Neither of the two provides an opportunity to explore the issues in detail and each restricts the responses through closed questions or limited interactional space (Grieshofer 2023a, 2023b).

To expand on the aforementioned list, the prominence of written genres and pre-court narratives illustrates the procedural burden put on court users (points (1) and (2)). Court forms in particular present a genre which can be confusing for parties mainly because of the lack of a coherent approach to their design, explanatory content (instructions on how to fill them in, procedural guidance, definitions of terms and concepts, links to legislation or practice directions), and their elicitation strategy (Grieshofer et al. 2021; Grieshofer 2023a). For instance, Grieshofer (2023a) details the shortcomings in the main form C100 used in child arrangements proceedings: from the layperson's perspective, the flaws include the lack of space for providing an initial narrative (lawyers would mainly include phrases with legal relevance – e.g. 'physical assault on [date]'), missing or decontextualised explanations of legal concepts and inaccurate framing of guidance (e.g. the framing of guidance implies that only women can be victims of domestic violence, or that abusive behaviour should not be mentioned if there is no evidence). Consequently, court forms completed by SRLs rarely present the full picture. Yet, court forms, as a genre for eliciting evidence, play a key role in determining the path the legal claim takes: based on the information presented in court forms, the judiciary and court staff decide whether the hearing is conducted in person or via a video link, if mediation is appropriate, what safeguarding or support measures are required, how urgent the first hearing is, who should the case be presided by (magistrates or a professional judge). Consequently, the minimal narratives elicited through the unfamiliar genre of court forms affect the narrativisation opportunities court users have during the rest of the proceedings (Grieshofer 2023a).

Similar difficulties apply to other pre-court genres. Interviews with advocates and SRLs illustrated a wide range of concerns related to preparing the documentation for court hearings. Advocates referred to conceptual, cognitive, discursive, procedural and legal difficulties: 'They don't understand the principles of law, even the welfare principle, and they don't understand how to present their case and how to conform to what is expected in terms of documents and disclosure and all of that' (B13); 'The skeleton arguments are often nonsense and just not worth looking at' (B2); 'They just do not understand the boundaries of evidence furnishing, evidence giving, and what they are allowed to submit and how they're allowed to interject at points' (B14). Similarly, court users expressed difficulties they experienced when preparing their evidence for court as they found it was not sufficient to simply present the facts as they saw them: 'Basically the biggest challenge is just how to fill the forms in and different things, really, that the solicitor would normally do' (LIP 6); 'That's the most difficult thing to begin with, preparing all the documentation in the right order, collating all the evidence together, doing it in a way that it's acceptable for court' (LIP 39); 'I thought it would be easy, I thought I just had the facts. If the facts were correct, I was either right or I was wrong' (LIP 10). It is the combination of several factors that makes the pre-court preparations especially daunting: procedural complexity, the need to comply with genre-specific requirements, the high number of diverse genres required, the adversarial nature of narratives elicited (see point (3) and Lee and Tkacukova 2016).

The first opportunity court users have to present a more detailed direct narration is through written witness statements, which is a specialised genre with clearly defined formal characteristics (numbered paragraphs, statement of truth, header with case number) and content (legally relevant arguments, compliance with procedural rules and practice directions). In three of the observed cases, the SRLs were asked to prepare a witness statement for the following hearings by following a template provided by the court. The template included information on formal characteristics (e.g. the header, statement of truth, numbers for numbered paragraphs), but there was no advice as to the purpose of witness statements, what is typically included or where to obtain help. Witness statements can be problematic even for lawyers: the quality and relevance of witness statements prepared by lawyers tends to vary significantly (Cooper and Mattison 2021). For many court users, the starting point is to at least understand what the genre is and how it is used, as illustrated in the following quote: 'Even when the judge said, 'You need a witness statement', I actually thought it's about witnesses, not about myself. I did not know' (LIP 22). Witness statements are one of many complex pre-court genres required from court users (see Tables 1 and 2). The complexity of the required multiple and diverse written genres raises the question of whether all of the procedural stages are essential (cf. Hunter et al. 2020, *Improving Access to Justice for Separating Families* 2022). Problem-solving courts, which shift the main emphasis towards the court users' engagement with the judiciary and the pre-allocated support team, illustrate that the simplification of pre-court procedures can be advantageous for parties and the system (*Problem-solving Courts* 2023).

An ancillary step of pre-court preparations is pre-court interviews with Cafcass, which are fraught with further problems (cf. Devine 2015; Newman 2010). The interviews are initially limited to closed questions to identify safeguarding risks and thus share similar issues to court forms due to the lack of open-enquiry approach; the short screening tests are thus conducted by officers who have very limited information about the circumstances of the case, and any information they have is based on the court form, which are flawed with elicitation deficiencies (Grieshofer 2023a). It is only section 7 interviews (section 7 of the Children Act 1989 – the report on the welfare of the child/children) that provide an opportunity for a more in-depth exploration of safeguarding concerns, but these investigations only apply to cases where the initial Cafcass interviews identify risks. The limited elicitation strategies contribute to risks being overlooked or misidentified (cf. Trinder et al. 2010). For instance, Trinder et al. (2010: 7) report on seven out of nine instances of court-based resolutions, in which allegations of domestic violence were marginalised and thus not explored or dealt with further. This illustrates the institutional biases that persevere across different contexts and become reflected in the poor design of discursive practices.

The further shortcoming of Cafcass investigations is that the interviews conducted with parents and children are not audio/video recorded. The institutional practice dictates that instead of recording the interviews, the officers make notes during the interviews. The dual role undoubtedly impedes on their ability to simultaneously engage with the interviewees and create a record of interviews for the subsequent report (cf. Gibb 2019). The lack of an audio recording means that it is not possible to trace what was originally said, which makes challenging Cafcass and social services' reports almost impossible. One of the consequences of this discursive practice is that challenging reports can have very little impact; lawyers, nevertheless, recognise that voicing the challenges can have a therapeutic effect on parents and thus follow their clients' instructions if they wish to exercise their right to contest social services' recommendations (Masson 2012). Inadvertently, the lack of recordings poses risks to the accuracy and overall quality of the reports. For instance, in six out of eleven observed hearings where a Cafcass report was discussed, there were factual inaccuracies and subjective interpretative comments (Grieshofer 2022b). The factual errors referred to wrong dates, types of offences or protective orders, frequencies of child contact, actions undertaken; some were simply not specific enough and showed that the assessment was not complete or the conclusions were not evidenced. For instance, one parent challenged the subjective description a Cafcass officer made in the report (describing the parent's home as 'grimy'); the Cafcass officer, who was present at the hearing, could not offer an explanation on why that remark was made, but insisted the house 'was not dirty, but grimy' (case 16). The written formats of evidence tend to be treated as final all-encompassing versions which are not open for discussion or challenge (cf. Haworth 2018). The high number of mistakes observed illustrates that the institutional practices require urgent changes. Addressing the deficiencies in institutional discursive practices and introducing more transparency into the interviewing, record-keeping, and reporting processes will help improve the currently tarnished image of Cafcass and social services and restore public trust in their assessments: there is a growing number of instances of children and their parents failed by the system and the corresponding negative portrayal of Cafcass services on social media and in press (cf. Hunter et al. 2020; Tickle 2019; Grieshofer 2022c; Tkacukova 2020). This unfortunately also affects the image of the family courts and translates into the distrust in the justice system from the most vulnerable in the society (Grieshofer 2022c).

As a genre, Cafcass reports are prone to discursive problems due to the inadequate collection and management of language data, despite the high significance attributed to them. It is not just the lack of audio recordings of original interactions and the resulting lack of transparency of the investigations. It is also the fact that social services and Cafcass officers collect the evidence from the parties without the presence of a lawyer (unlike during police interviews where the lawyer can be present) and the fact that their reports are trusted without being subject to institutional quality assurance processes or research-based scrutiny (see point (5)): elicitation processes are not explored, the record keeping processes are unclear, the report writing stage relies on notes and memory without an inquiry into data/evidence interpretation methods (cf. Grieshofer 2022b, 2023b). Yet, the reports have an adjudicative function and the judiciary are likely to enforce the recommendations made by social services or Cafcass as the statutory body (cf. Hunter 2007). It is also important to bear in mind that when writing the reports, officers have to present and defend their opinions with the view of being cross-examined. The reports are thus a product of the adversarial approach (*Separate Representation of Children* 2006) and presenting the views of children or their parents accurately is not their primary objective. There is a possibility that the adversarial undertone of the reports weakens their investigative and exploratory function (cf. Grieshofer 2023b; Devine 2015). The adjudicative role of Cafcass reports thus needs to be explored further within the context of the proceedings and procedural justice.

The court procedures continuously limit the narrativisation scope of individual hearings and the parties' satellite narratives. It is the applicant/claimant who create the story first in pre-court stages and the respondents thus have to respond by reframing the applicant's/claimant's story, proposing a different interpretation and reacting to pre-defined topics, and as a result, the respondents have few opportunities to propose new topics. The reduction in narrativisation scope occurs throughout the proceedings for different reasons (see point (7)): pre-court satellite narratives limit the satellite narratives in court; the aim of individual hearings limits the topics which can be covered; the interim court orders and directions limit the scope of pre-court narratives. Court users thus do not have an opportunity to share the full version of their stories and the continuous need to refocus and reinterpret their narratives breaks the coherence of the internal structure of their narratives (cf. Tkacukova 2016). In theory, the reduction in scope could potentially strengthen the legal relevance of the parties' narratives, but this potential cannot be realised unless the parties are supported in understanding the decision-making principles applicable to their situation (cf. Holt and Thompson 2023). In practice, the risk is that some legally relevant narrativisation threads can be lost due to the institutional culture (e.g. the pro-contact culture) or court users not communicating them clearly (Grieshofer 2023b).

It is mainly in the interactive and open-enquiry formats that court users find it easier to present their narratives (cf. Grieshofer 2023b; Lee and Tkacukova 2017; Trinder et al. 2014). When it comes to hearings, court users expect to have their day in court and have their stories heard. But the initial hearings are predominantly procedural and it is mainly lawyers, the judiciary and experts who are asked to contribute to procedural aspects (see points (4), (6) and (8)). In private family proceedings in England and Wales, there is thus very limited opportunity (if at all) for litigants to present their stories and it is not until the final hearing that their narratives can be heard in court as part of witness examination (especially the examination-in-chief part). But, as previously mentioned, many child-related proceedings do not reach the final hearing due to a wide range of reasons: institutional pressure to settle out of court, the realisation that Cafcass reports define the outcomes, long duration of the proceedings (cf. Grieshofer 2023b; Hunter et al. 2020; *Improving Access to Justice for Separating Families* 2022). And in those cases that reach the final hearing, the scope of the narratives will have been narrowed down through all the procedural stages. It is thus not surprising that court users feel they are not being heard (cf. Hunter et al. 2020), as reflected in interviews with SRLs: 'You know what I would like to see? To have the opportunity to express yourself (. . .) Straightaway, you are shut up in the sense of, "No time, not now"' (LIP 22); 'The decisions were kind of made for [us]. It just felt a little bit like it wasn't very inclusive' (LIP 1). The procedural focus of initial hearings, alongside the prevalence of written genres, is the result of recent court reforms which prioritised procedural complexity and weakened the principle of orality (cf. Lazer 2021).

The lack of discursive competence and procedural experience makes it difficult for court users to present their cases in the manner that is procedurally acceptable. As the narratives move from the case management stage (usually during the first two hearings) to submissions (the fact-finding and final hearings), the challenge is to present a coherent narrative first through the pre-hearing documentation (e.g. documents, court forms, statements) and then through written and oral testimony (e.g. witness statements, witness examination), which builds on the documentation and creates persuasive arguments. As one advocate pointed out in the interview: 'What I would say about [SRLs] is that the most problem that they face is in what I would call directions type hearings, as in not in evidence, because of course they don't understand how to play the game or how to say things as they should be said' (B11). The directions hearings concern with evidence rather than submissions and so in some types of hearings (e.g. financial remedy proceedings discussed in the following section), the judiciary are able to assess the strength of the parties' cases on the basis of the documentation provided. In child arrangements proceedings, directions hearings allow the parties to raise issues but not expand on them (e.g. it is important to present the issue, such as 'the child does get quite upset when they come back from the contact' instead of listing problems 'the child cried', 'the child didn't want to go'). Yet, as previously established, it is mainly in response to open initiations and open-enquiry interactions with the judiciary or other legal professionals that SRLs are more likely to present their cases more efficiently (Trinder et al. 2014). The extent to which they receive this opportunity depends, in the first instance, on the judiciary: the judiciary define how and when court users can express themselves (within the limits of the court hearing communicative objectives). Once the court user is provided with an opportunity to speak, it then depends on them to what extent they are able to express their voice.

In theoretical and applied linguistics, the concept of voice entails the physical ability to project the voice, the manner in which the projection happens, and whether the audience perceives the projection favourably (cf. Heffer 2013).

The term voice projection draws on Hymes' (1996) idea that in order for the voice to be heard in a specific context, it needs to be accepted and valued. Therefore, the voice can only be successfully projected if all the conditions are met: the voice is allowed to be expressed, the input is welcome, the voice projection opportunity is taken, the stylistic characteristics are context appropriate and the input is accepted (cf. Heffer 2013, 2018; Grieshofer 2022b). In the context of child-related proceedings, the first two conditions depend on whether the scope and objective of a hearing allow for the voice to be projected, which topics the procedural stage allows to be discussed or introduced and, to some extent, whether the hearing is before a judge or magistrates.

For instance, at one FHDRA (First Hearing Dispute Resolution Appointment – see Table 1) with both parents present as SRLs (case 10), the district judge spent most of the hearing explaining where the case stands (Parent 2 applied for a non-molestation order against Parent 1; Cafcass recommendation was to prepare the section 7 report due to safeguarding concerns; the question remained whether there should be any contact between Parent 1 and child while the safeguarding investigations were being completed). The judge was clear in their opinion as to what the next steps should be: 'I am conscious not to take away contact [of Parent 1] with child. What I can do is put in place an interim order which will say that contact is at Cafcass' discretion.' Once the judge has set out their position, only Parent 2 (as a residing parent) was asked for their input: '[Parent 2], do you have anything to add?' At that point, the parent asked for a clarification on the Cafcass recommendations and the interim order, which led to judge providing further explanation: 'It will be at the discretion of the social worker and they would decide if seeing [the child] is possible and how to see the child.' Parent 1 was not asked to contribute, but they managed to interrupt and ask a question: 'So they won't let me see [the child]?' The Cafcass officer present at the hearing responded to the question by explaining the procedure and saying that 'on initial appointment, it will be important to consider what contact there is to happen' and the judge proceeded to offer some reassurance: 'As of today, there has been good involvement of Cafcass. [Addressing the Cafcass officer], I will get the order out quickly, so that they do not have to wait for three months until the next hearing. [Addressing the parties], the court now has to be guided by experts in safeguarding.' When Parent 2 attempted to expand on their case ('I would like to add more about how [Parent 1] treats me and [child]'), the judge halted this specific topic by saying: 'This is something to say at the final hearing.'

What can be drawn from the observation (case 10) is that the hearing was well-structured, which was found to be the case with all observed hearings presided by the professional judiciary: it progressed from the overview of issues to be resolved to the procedural steps to be taken and offering explanation and reassurance (e.g. as to the timing of the court order, avoiding unnecessary delays for the safeguarding assessment and the next hearing). Both parents received an opportunity to ask questions, though it was mainly the residing parent's views which were actively elicited. Given the stage of the proceedings and the procedurally limited communicative objective of the hearing, the parents could not project their voices (beyond asking questions), expand on any of the topics or provide evidence. The fact that the Cafcass assessment was given a decisive role in how the case developed also reduced the relevance of anything the parents could contribute at that point. In sum, the judge was accommodating to the parties' needs and concerns (e.g. by expressing the hesitance to take the contact away), but neither of the parties could be given an opportunity (by the judge and court procedures) to contribute substantially due to the procedural and communicative aims of the FHDRA hearing.

In another hearing (case 6), both SRL parents were given an opportunity to project their voices, but their turns did not have a significant impact on the outcome of the hearing. The hearing was attended by a Cafcass officer and presided by three magistrates who were supported by a legal adviser (the role of legal advisers is to assist magistrates with legal matters). As a result, there were five participants with a powerful institutional role and two SRLs whose opinions were elicited but who had to compete for interactional space and were limited in the extent to which they could contribute and how their contributions were interpreted. The hearing was planned as a final hearing of the case which lasted for over a year and the only contested issue left to be resolved was whether the child should have contact with Parent 2 (the living arrangements were previously confirmed with Parent 1). Both the Cafcass officer and Parent 1 verified that the child did not wish to have contact with Parent 2 as a consequence of multiple issues with the conduct and lack of reliability of Parent 2. This was clarified by the legal adviser at the beginning of the hearing:

> Legal adviser (to Parent 1): Is it your position that the child does not want to spend time with [Parent 2]?
> Parent 1: Yes.
> Legal adviser (to the Cafcass officer): To the best of your knowledge, is it true?
> Cafcass officer: Yes.

But what subsequently happened was a shift from this clear position: at the initiation of the Presiding Justice (i.e. the magistrate chairing the hearing), the magistrates and the legal adviser prompted the Cafcass officer if there were any options left to support the chid in regaining interest in contact: 'What would be the effect of telling [child] that [pronoun for child] would not see [Parent 2] now?' (legal adviser); 'As a therapeutic exercise, it can be positive to think about additional options for child-focussed sessions' (Presiding Justice).

Eventually, the Cafcass officer joined the magistrates and the legal adviser in persuading Parent 1 to try one more time to support the contact between the child and Parent 2. The discussion, led by the Presiding Justice and legal adviser, displayed several characteristics: it was happening in an unstructured way as they kept covering different options and then coming back to them; in the process of doing so, they combined explanatory and persuasive turns with questions eliciting the opinions of the parents; their prompts shifted from hypothetical tentative discussion points to more resolute decisions (e.g. from 'Would you be willing?' to '[Parent] agrees'). Throughout the hearing, opinions of Parent 1 were repeatedly sought:

> Legal adviser: How do you feel about this decision?
> Parent 1: I'm sick it's been so long. (...) Now it is just pressure, I don't want that anymore. I'll do whatever you tell me, but I don't agree.
> Presiding Justice: Would you be willing?
> Parent 1: I feel like it's pressure on [child].
> (...)
> Cafcass officer: If [child] wanted to have contact, [child] should be able to. (...) Cafcass will do a piece of work with parents and the child. Parents don't need to like each other and it's about parenting. We need to find out [child's] wishes, so the programme is for that. At the end of the day, if you can't, you can't do anything.
> Parent 1: Just because everyone sat here thinks that it's a good idea, it doesn't mean it's a good idea for [child].

In the end, reservations of Parent 1 were not heard and the position of Parent 1 was simply summarised as '[Parent 1] says [pronoun for Parent 1] will promote it and is willing to give this one more chance' (Presiding Justice), which also meant that the hearing was changed to an interim hearing and another final hearing was scheduled for a later date. Interestingly, Parent 2 remained mostly silent for the majority of the hearing. When the problematic conduct of Parent 2 was brought up, the parent simply admitted their fault:

> Presiding Justice: Explain yourself! What were you thinking? Telling [age]-year-old that you are dropping the proceedings and then coming back to court? You weren't thinking of [child]. It's a stupid thing to do. Now you're here wanting a chance.
> Parent 2: I'm embarrassed. It was a mistake.

Apart from scolding Parent 2, the magistrates and legal adviser steered the discussion in the way that did not require participation from Parent 2 and they only elicited their consent to participate in the programme ('Presiding Justice: Would you be willing? / Parent 2: Yes'). This development and outcome of the hearing corresponds with the institutional narrative of promoting contact between parents and children, even in situations when the previous attempts continuously failed and the child no longer wishes to participate in programmes or see a parent (cf. Hunter et al. 2020). Paradoxically, at the end of the hearing, reservations of Parent 1 are muted, whereas Parent 2 is encouraged by the Presiding Justice ('Don't worry too much. Cooperate and, hopefully, it is not too difficult'), which shows that the negative impact of the institutional narrative can turn into the imbalance in responsibilities when it comes to the effort expected from the resident parents as opposed to non-resident parents (cf. Hunter et al. 2020). The power imbalance between the institutional roles of the participants, an exploratory approach to finding options which could still be explored through Cafcass, and the institutionally and discursively powerful function shared among the magistrates, legal adviser and Cafcass officer led to the situation when the eliciting strategy (with the embedded explanation, persuasion and scolding) was used to support the court agenda and mute the voices of the child and the resident parent.

In yet another case (case 2), the DRA (Directions/Dispute Resolution Appointment) hearing was presided by three magistrates and a legal adviser and attended by the applicant SRL Parent 1 and the residing Parent 2 who was represented by a solicitor. The floor was initially given to the SRL Parent 1 to present the summary of the case: 'It's your application, so you can start' (Presiding Justice). But the solicitor for Parent 2 interrupted by saying: 'I talked to [Parent1], so it may be better if I address the court.' The Presiding Justice accepted this and explained that normally an applicant would start, but on this occasion, it would be the solicitor who starts. In semi-represented cases, the judiciary tend to allow a lawyer to present the summary of the case, even if they are representing a respondent and the overview of the case is meant to be presented by an applicant (cf. Trinder et al. 2014; Tkacukova 2010; Wangmann et al. 2020). From the communicative perspective, the party who starts the summary defines which topics would be discussed and how they would be framed (Grieshofer 2022b). Despite the advocates' overriding duty to the court and the Law Society's ethics code requiring legal representatives to be especially careful in their communication in semi-represented cases (*Litigants in person: Guidelines for lawyers* 2015), the author observed legal representatives occasionally framing their clients' version as the preferred one (e.g. see the discussion of case 34 in the next section). By taking an opportunity to summarise the case, the solicitor presented that their client was not happy with the section 7 report and its recommendations (due to misleading information, discrepancy between what the report said and the evidence it covered, inconsistencies within the report, missing information), arguing that the contact arrangements recommended in the report were not safe. As the solicitor talked at length, the SRL Parent 1 interrupted them and took the opportunity to express their agreement with the report's recommendations, despite its inconsistencies: 'I didn't know anything about [child's needs identified by Parent 2], so news to me as well.' This initiated a series of interruptions by the represented client and the SRL parent, despite the Presiding Justice's request to the represented client: 'You need to let applicant [Parent] talk.' As a result, the SRL Parent 1 managed to put forward several narrativisation threads expressed in short sentences at different points during the hearing (possibly due to the fact that their turns were reduced by interruptions): 'I've proved I'm not a threat. I want to see my child'; '[Parent 2] doesn't want me to see my [child]'; 'I'm not a risk'; 'It's frustrating, my family didn't see the [child] for [number] years'; 'Even if [pronoun for child] is [special needs], I'm still [child's parent] and want contact'. At the end of the hearing, the recommendation the magistrates made was for contact to proceed on the condition that the child's needs are considered during contact and the contact arrangements to be reviewed after three contacts. In sum, despite the interruption from the other party, limited elicitation from the judiciary and opposition voiced by the advocate for the other party, the SRL parent managed to obtain the outcome they wished for, thanks to several factors: (1) the Cafcass recommendations for contact; (2) the pro-contact institutional culture; (3) self-created opportunities for voice projection; (4) the clarity of the SRL's narrativisation threads. Although the first two factors undoubtedly played a decisive role in the outcome of the hearing, the other two aspects contributed to ensuring the SRL was given an opportunity to see the child without any delays and that the contact arrangements were framed in a flexible manner (i.e. the contact could proceed beyond the three initial visits, based on a review opportunity which was not formally defined as a Cafcass review or court review).

A similar interaction strategy did not work for an SRL Parent 2 who faced a represented applicant Parent 1 at a DRA hearing (case 16). Despite interrupting and taking the floor whenever possible and despite managing to introduce and address critical issues in relation to the well-being of the child, the SRL parent's wishes for more contact, and for contact to be unsupervised, were not heard. The narrative threads presented by the SRL parent in fragmented threads included important arguments directly relevant to the welfare principle and rationale for unsupervised contact: '[Child pronoun] has [special needs], so if the supervising officer is late or doesn't get on with [child pronoun], it messes everything up'; '[Parent 1] doesn't understand the needs and the [child] isn't registered for school'. Nevertheless, the SRL was not consistent in the narrative and introduced multiple irrelevant narrativisation threads (e.g. the needs of their new partner). The other issue was that their request for contact was not in agreement with the Cafcass report, so the chances of the contact being planned according to the parent's wishes were minimal and the unclear narrativisation strategy with irrelevant details was only to the detriment of their case. What was unusual was that the SRL parent could only proceed with the supervised contact, despite not being identified as a safeguarding risk. The only reason mentioned was related to the fact that the child was once aggressive towards the SRL parent, but neither the Cafcass report nor the magistrates expanded further on the rationale behind supervised contact, despite the SRL's requests for clarification. While the SRL's voice projection opportunities were limited due to the procedural stage of the case, the lack of explanation on how the contact decision was reached undoubtedly further limited the parent's options in contextualising their arguments.

Although the SRL kept offering different arguments and starting different narrativisation threads, they were continuously interrupted by the legal advisor and the Presiding Justice as the narrative did not fit with the procedural and communicative aims of the hearing, which also meant that the magistrates or the legal adviser did not attempt to elicit the narrative in a more structured manner. Instead, to follow court procedures, the legal adviser asked the parent to prepare their narrative in the form of a witness statement for the following hearing. To introduce the idea of the witness statement, the parent was simply given a template. Upon reviewing the SRLs' options for gaining legal assistance and establishing that it was not financially affordable, the Presiding Justice and legal adviser tried to help with the content of the witness statement at different points in the hearing: 'focus on the child', 'explain why you'd be a better parent', 'this is what you need to do is to put everything [about household and special needs] in the statement', 'if you are concerned about contact notes and if you had a solicitor, you'd want to say you don't want notes, but witnesses instead – other observers and include people's contacts'. Despite the magistrates' efforts to offer some guidance, the fact that the court procedures only allow for the elicitation of evidence through the written genre meant that the parent was left confused and possibly in a much weaker position than they would have been if their narrative had been elicited in a structured interactive format.

All four cases discussed here illustrate that the extent to which court users are successful with having their voices heard is defined by the following factors: the stage of the proceedings they are in, whether the parties' expectations and requests are reasonable, whether the judiciary give opportunities for voice projection or that opportunity is successfully taken, whether the parties' arguments are in line with Cafcass recommendations and whether the arguments proposed align with the overarching institutional narrative. The child arrangements proceedings are replete with discursive barriers due to the fact that parties are not given many opportunities to project their voices in the initial stages of the proceedings and, instead, they are sent out of court to complete forms, write witness statements and talk to social services. Throughout the duration of the proceedings, court users are thus continuously denied an opportunity to tell their stories before the judge, until the stage of the final hearing, and even then their voice is not always heard and the institutional narrative can override the children and parents' wishes (cf. Hunter et al. 2020).

7 Discursive Practices in Financial Remedy Proceedings

Financial remedy proceedings are legal proceedings which deal with ex-partners' finances as part of a divorce or dissolution of a civil partnership. In comparison to child arrangements cases, the discursive practices embedded in financial remedy proceedings are arguably more complex when it comes to pre-court narrativisation and evidence provision, but at the same time they are potentially more manageable and accessible when it comes to court hearings. The complexity of pre-court stages lies in comprehension-related and discursive challenges faced by many court users when attempting to complete court forms and subsequently producing coherent narratives through numerical arguments (e.g. the narrative on financial needs – *Guidance on 'Financial Needs' on Divorce* 2016). But once these pre-court stages in relation to full disclosure of financial situation of both parties are completed satisfactorily, the court hearings are essentially managed in a more inquisitorial manner as the court is not bound by the evidence submitted by the parties and has a duty to investigate any outstanding matters (*The Family Court Practice*: Part 9, section 9.15; Black et al. 2014). As a result, the judiciary tend to actively elicit evidence and provide more support with narrativisation. This is reflected in the communicative aims of individual hearings and the progression of the proceedings from case management to defining the likely outcome and identifying acceptable solutions before the contested final hearing (see Table 2).

Table 2 presents the blueprint of what is expected to happen during the financial remedy proceedings, focusing on the genres and aims of pre-court and court stages. The actual proceedings may differ due to the level of readiness of the pre-court stages: for instance, the first directions appointment (FDA) and financial dispute resolution (FDR) hearings may be combined if full disclosure is complied with and there is no further evidence from evaluation experts required, or an extra interim hearing may be added if the questionnaires need

Table 2 Narrativisation in financial remedy applications (according to 'Family Procedure Rules – Part 9').

Pre-hearing stages

Narrative genres	Narration
Communicative goal: initiating proceedings, comply with disclosures	
Form A (procedural, adversarial)	Direct (parties or lawyer)
Form E (procedural, adversarial)	Direct (parties or lawyer)
Chronology of key dates (procedural)	Direct (parties or lawyer)
Questionnaire (procedural, adversarial)	Direct (parties or lawyer)
Summary of the issues in the case (procedural, adversarial)	Direct (parties or lawyer)
	All narrations
Communicative goal: preparing evidence	
Questionnaire (procedural, adversarial)	Direct (parties or lawyer)
Proposal for settlement (procedural, adversarial, adjudicative)	Direct (parties or lawyer)
Summary of the issues in the case (procedural, adversarial)	Direct (parties or lawyer)
Court bundle (procedural, adversarial)	All narrations
Communicative goal: preparing further evidence	
Witness statements	Direct, antagonistic (applicant, then respondent)
Court bundle (procedural, adversarial)	All narrations

Court hearings

Narrative genres	Narration
First Directions Appointment (FDA) **Communicative goal:** case management, ensuring disclosures are complied with, identifying issues	
Out-of-court negotiations	Direct (parties) or lawyer-mediated
Presenting the case/position (adversarial)	Direct (parties) or lawyer-framed
Case management and narrowing down issues (procedural, adversarial, adjudicative)	Judge-mediated (judge and parties or their lawyers)
Directions (procedural, adjudicative)	Directive for further expert evidence and narrative scope (judiciary)
Financial Dispute Resolution Appointment (FDR) **Communicative goal:** judge giving an indication as to a reasonable solution and likely outcomes, encourage negotiations	
Out-of-court negotiations	Direct (parties) or lawyer-mediated
Presenting the case/position (adversarial)	Direct (parties) or lawyer-framed
Case management and narrowing down issues (procedural, adversarial, adjudicative)	Judge-mediated (judge and parties or their lawyers)
Directions (procedural, adjudicative)	Directive for further evidence and narrative scope (judiciary)
Financial Dispute Resolution hearing **Communicative goal:** conduct contested trial, determine the outcome	
Presenting the case/position (adversarial)	Direct (parties) or lawyer-framed
Case management and narrowing down issues (procedural, adversarial, adjudicative)	Judge-mediated (judge and parties or their lawyers)
Witness examination (adversarial)	Direct and lawyer-framed (parties, lawyers, judiciary)
Financial Remedy Order	Directive for post-proceedings stage (judge)

to be revisited after the FDA hearing (e.g. to remove questions due to their irrelevance or inappropriateness).

All pre-court genres are direct narratives in the form of court forms or idiosyncratic genres specific for this type of proceedings. The court forms are particularly complex due to (1) the fact that they draw on two specialised discourses, legal discourse and financial discourse, (2) ambiguous syntactic and grammatical complexity and missing coherence links, and (3) incomplete instructions and confusing layout. For instance, Form A functions as an introductory form for the subsequent Form E, which is longer and more complex. Tkacukova (2016) details the linguistic challenges present in Form A, where even the first section complicates comprehension by drawing on concepts from law and finance, introduces ambiguity by using double negation and several conditionals within the same sentence, breaks the coherence of the main clause through the bullet point sections, creates visual obstacles by including multiple meta-textual references and links and unnecessarily includes redundant options for court orders that litigants may not be aware of at the beginning of the proceedings. What is largely missing in Forms A and E is an accessible and comprehensible definition of terms, instructions on how to fill in the forms or where to find the information in pay slips or pension statements or even procedural guidance and explanation of key judicial decision-making principles. Unlike legislative texts, where there is a risk of reducing explicitness and specificity in case of linguistic simplifications (Bhatia and Bhatia 2011), the court forms used in financial remedy proceedings can be simplified without the risk of reducing accuracy as many of the question categories relate to the numbers; linguistic improvements, including clear exemplification and elicitation, will be particularly advantageous for lay court users (cf. the improvements provided in the C100 form discussed by Grieshofer 2023a). As court application processes move online, it is especially important to invest in the clarity of elicitation and information provision practices, given that the digitised formats are encouraging, and often even presuming, that court users are completing the forms independently even if they are planning to seek legal advice at a later stage (cf. Grieshofer 2023a).

The hearings observed as part of the study showed that all court users struggled with completing the forms or providing all the evidence to a satisfactory level. For instance, in one FDA hearing (case 24) with both parties representing themselves, there were only minor gaps in some categories (omissions in 'other assets', such as a car or jewellery). In another FDA hearing, the SRL applicant did not fill in the Form E or bring any other documents and the respondent did not engage with the proceedings at all (case 23). Even FDR hearings indicated patchy pre-court preparations: in one hearing, the SRL respondent did not produce Form E and did not comply with full disclosure of bank statements (case 34); in other cases, some aspects were left out (parts of Form E in case 39, not all directions complied with in the same case 39, missing evidence of child maintenance arrears in case 17). Most of these issues are due to the fact that the elicitation of evidence is not clear and that it can be time-consuming to locate all the supporting evidence required for the final hearing. Even if the parties do not contest the issue, the documents still need to be provided for procedural reasons, which can be demotivating for court users. On occasion, SRLs' lack of procedural understanding and discursive difficulties are further compounded by their mistrust towards the opposing party and their lawyers, resulting in intentional non-disclosure of documents; such attitudinal barriers (cf. McKeever et al. 2018) are only exacerbated if the discursive practices are problematic and informational justice tenets are not fulfilled in the pre-court stages. For instance, the reason the SRL respondent did not submit their bank statements in case 34 was because they did not understand the concept of full disclosure and did not want the other party and their solicitor to see the bank statements. The feelings of mistrust are very common in semi-represented cases (cf. Trinder et al. 2014; Lee and Tkacukova 2017; Tkacukova 2020) and it is important that the pre-court information provision addresses the court users' lack of confidence in the system by ensuring the guidance is easy to find, presented in a coherent manner through the use of everyday language, and addresses common misconceptions and biases (cf. Grieshofer 2022c).

Despite the challenges presented with paperwork, the judiciary adopted a very pragmatic approach in all of the observed hearings: they guided the parties through the court procedures, provided a detailed explanation of what law says about issues relevant to the case, and indicated the legal principles relevant to the judicial decision-making processes. At the FDA level, it was predominantly procedural information provided alongside the encouragement to engage with the process further. In case 23, where the respondent did not appear before court or engage with the proceedings and the SRL applicant did not fill in Form E, the judge introduced the purpose of the proceedings and explained how the challenge of non-attendance could be addressed: 'In order for court to do this, the court needs full disclosure from both parties. At this hearing, the idea is that you'd have filled in Form E and then you raise a questionnaire asking for further questions. Then we have full disclosure and we are in the position to give full directions'; 'If [ex-partner] doesn't comply, then we can arrest and force [ex-partner] to comply'; 'Let's say [ex-partner] isn't here next time. So what court sometimes can do is list for a final hearing and then just make decision on your documents (. . .) but we have to give [ex-partner] that opportunity'; 'You'll be fine once you come to the final hearing. You just need to comply with the order'. The explanation and reassurance provided by the judge helped address the party's concerns about the non-engagement and non-attendance of the other party and provided clarity on the options available.

Similarly, in case 24, the judge checked the documentation and forms and helped the self-represented parties to construct their narratives through prompting the line of reasoning and eliciting additional information from them:

> Judge: Who lives in the former matrimonial home?
> Parent 2: Me.
> Judge: Where does the child live?
> Parent 1: With me.
> (. . .)
> Judge: Are you arguing that anyone is entitled to more?
> Parent 1: Yes, I.
> Judge: Why?
> Parent 1: Because of the child.
> (. . .)
> Judge: (To Parent 2) You say, I should get more because [Parent 1] lives with a new partner. (To Parent 1) You say, I need to get more because I am looking after [child].

Exemplifying the narrativisation strategies the parties should pursue presents a particularly helpful type of discursive practice. The judge was also checking the viability of the situation and potential solutions ('Do you accept the house should be sold?'; 'Is somebody struggling to pay the mortgage?'), conducting case management ('For FDR, are you able to agree an evaluation now?') and managing expectations while encouraging the parties to negotiate ('Nothing stops you from negotiating and trying to come to a solution. If you leave it to the judge, it could be that you are really unhappy about it. (. . .) A clean break is always better'). The support was offered through effective elicitation strategies, narrativisation advice and the provision of clear procedural and legal information. This type of judiciary style clearly deviates from the typical adversarial approach and shows potential for discursive effectiveness, though the pre-court procedural complexity still remains a negative consequence of adversarialism.

What works particularly well in financial remedy proceedings is that at the stage of FDR hearings, the role of the judiciary is to provide the indication of the likely solutions possible as well as evaluate the weaknesses and strengths of the parties' financial situation (cf. Holt and Thomson 2023). This allows the judge to adopt a more problem-solving approach to the dispute resolution (cf. *Problem-solving courts: An evidence review* 2019) and express their opinion fully. To retain the judicial objectivity within the proceedings, the judge from the FDR hearing is never listed for the final hearing. The practice of the judiciary providing directions and evaluating the strengths and weaknesses of the cases is beneficial for not only the parties but also the legal system and different stages of the proceedings (including the mediation stage – cf. Hitchings and Miles 2016; Holt and Thomson 2023). It is mainly at the FDR stage that this benefit is fully embraced by the judiciary who evaluate the positions of parties and encourage negotiations. Given the clearly defined institutional role of the FDR judges, their messages are uniform and perform several functions:

1. Explaining their role – 'I am here to help you to understand the process' (case 17); 'I am going to talk to you to see what it is you dispute' (case 17); 'I told you today what your chances are. I cannot tell you what to put in your evidence' (case 17).

2. Encouraging the parties to negotiate and settle – 'I can settle in nine out of ten cases. Any reason I should not settle this case?' (case 17); 'I will look at [Applicant's] evidence and your evidence and then I will say you are going to win that or not and encourage settlement before the final hearing' (case 17); '[the advantage of negotiating is] end of uncertainty, minimising the cost of litigation comes out of [family budget], nobody can be happy if matters are left to the judge' (case 34); 'it is not a binding decision, just an indication of what advantage there is for you to agree and then you have more control' (case 34).

3. Discouraging the parties from the final hearing – 'If the case goes to the final hearing, then the decision is imposed on you' (case 34); 'you will have stress and the trial won't take place until [eight months' time]' (case 17); '(to the solicitor) I strongly urge your client takes this on board, it is cheaper to do it now rather than pay legal fees' (case 17); 'you shouldn't go to court for that point, it needs to be dealt with' (case 17); 'be pragmatic, come to an agreement' (case 17).

The functional uniformity and presentation style (use of simple everyday language) is part of the judiciary's powerful discursive strategy for providing support and enhancing court users' understanding of relevant legal aspects: as a result, most proceedings are, in fact, settled during or after the FDR (Hitchings et al. 2014).

The fact that court users are offered substantial support with evaluating the strengths and weaknesses of their cases becomes even more significant when taking into account that financial remedy proceedings incorporate two ongoing narrativisation threads: the narrative of the parties' financial situation and the fairness narrative framed and interpreted through legal, financial and societal criteria. While the financial needs are elicited through court forms, the second narrativisation thread relies on such unusual genres as questionnaires, summaries of the issues and witness statements. The elicitation of the second type of narratives and their framing is supported by the judiciary in court hearings. What is of interest with this type of narratives is that this is where the parties' societal values and expectations, often based on family roles, collide; the strength of arguments and narratives proposed is thus defined through socio-legal norms. The fairness in financial remedy proceedings is judged according to the principles of needs, compensation and sharing (Heenan 2018). But these principles are dependent on how the media, society and courts view marriage. The prevailing view among socio-legal scholars is that interdependency is an inherent part of marriage as an institution, and courts should fully acknowledge the financial and career sacrifices made by those spouses who become primary child carers or assume other house-hold responsibilities. In court, it is then important to establish the narrative, which ensures the entitlement of the economically weaker spouse to the appropriate financial support post-divorce (Heenan 2018; Miles and Hitchings 2018).

This is exemplified at the FDR hearing (case 34), where the parties disagreed about each other's financial needs arguments and whether an older child, a university student, needed to be part of the needs assessment. The SRL Parent 2 claimed that 'one child at uni and full-time student, back for odd weekends, is not a factor when it comes to needs', whereas the solicitor for Parent 1 argued that 'students still need a place' as 'the general policy is for students to have a roof' and the judge confirmed that 'students' needs is still a factor'. Further arguments about the financial needs of the parties were framed through social factors by the solicitor when showing the photos of the accommodation chosen by the SRL parent for the residing parent: 'Young professionals at this day and age stay at home until they are fully qualified', 'this is what [Parent 2] proposes for [pronoun for Parent 2] former [spouse] and [pronoun for Parent 2] children. I am sure humans live there, but it is under bedroom tax – smaller than (. . .) this bedroom is not much wider than I am tall. It seems that what [Parent 2] has done is propose a 50/50 share. That can't be right. It's a step down on a property ladder. It's perfectly right and proper to be not in the ex-housing accommodation, near the school, in decent condition'. The SRL's response focused more on personal needs and thus was not successful:

> I've chosen to live in [new area]. I'm employed there. [New area] is more expensive than [current area]. (. . .) The houses I chose for [Parent 1] were in the range of [prices], when [Parent 1] did not have a mortgage ranging capacity. There are two-bedroom houses elsewhere in respectable areas, in good areas, not excessive but close to school. I chose the area for myself where we holidayed so that [children] could come stay with me over the summer.

The outcome of the hearing was that the judge encouraged the parties to negotiate while managing the expectations of Parent 2: 'The main residence will be with [Parent 1] and likely to visit [Parent 2], but secondary to primary needs. Not right to allocate more to [spousal role of Parent 2] than [Parent 1] and children.' Narrativisation is thus built and challenged on the basis of societal roles and expectations and the framing of the narratives can help establish their socio-legal relevance.

Another related issue is the degree to which courts should be proactive in cases in which the narrative may potentially be dominated by an abusive partner. Currently, abusive behaviour does not have an impact on the financial remedy claims, but it is important to recognise that controlling behaviour impacts the narrative of the proceedings and establish to which degree it had an impact on past financial decisions, career development and the resulting future financial sustainability of individuals (Crisp et al. 2022). Crisp et al. (2022) argue that clarifying the statutory definition of coercive or controlling behaviour would enable legal professionals to reduce the impact abuse has on the proceedings. For instance, at the FDA hearing (case 23), where the respondent did not engage and the applicant raised domestic abuse allegations, the judge explained that it was not relevant:

> You might want to raise this, but however nasty the behaviour was, it is very rarely relevant to the court decision. I am not belittling you, but being a horrible [spouse] is not enough. We need you to focus on the money and fair distribution of the money. Don't bring issues from [abusive email], focus on money. (. . .) You're entitled to 50/50, but depends on other factors, such as health and so on. The court can take it into account if you provide evidence.

Despite the fact that allegations and non-engagement pointed to wider domestic violence issues, including potentially financial abuse, the judge doubted that these could be factored in. Nevertheless, it can be important for courts to consider domestic abuse as a further factor in the financial needs analysis (e.g. if someone is not engaging in selling assets, the assets may lose value, impacting the finances of both parties), especially in cases where the abuse is evidenced and the abusive partner denies an opportunity for the victim to even project their voice (cf. Crisp at el. 2022).

Overall, the parties in the observed financial remedy proceedings (represented and unrepresented parties) were offered substantial support from the judiciary who tended to adopt a problem-solving approach and helped court users not only understand the decision-making principles but also frame their financial needs narratives. Interestingly, court users were mainly restricted to responding to questions, but that also meant that their voices were mostly projected effectively and the information was relevant to the needs analysis arguments. During the hearings, the discursive practices thus accommodated legal and lay discursive differences and the function of the FDR hearing was found to be particularly helpful in establishing the relevant narrativisation threads and identifying the strengths and weaknesses of the parties' cases. The effectiveness of such hearings is recognised by legal professionals: there have recently been appeals issued to introduce resolution hearings in child arrangements proceedings (Holt and Thomson 2023) to ensure the judiciary can be more forthcoming in communicating the relevant legal and procedural principles at the heart of their decision-making processes. What remains to be a barrier for court users in financial remedy proceedings is the gap in informational justice due to the procedural and discursive complexity of pre-court written genres, which essentially mute SRLs' voices in the initial stages of the proceedings (Grieshofer 2023a). The further issue which needs to be addressed is defining abuse and its impact on the parties' discursive competencies in presenting their cases in and out of court stages as well as ensuring that the courts can provide a fair treatment to anyone economically disadvantaged (Heenan 2018).

8 Discursive Practices in County Courts

County courts deal with the majority of civil litigation cases, which include money claims and small claims cases, personal injury claims, housing claims, bankruptcy and insolvency matters. In 2021, 89 per cent of 1.58 million received claims were claims for money, but the majority (83 per cent of the received claims) was settled without the need for a hearing (*Court statistics for England and Wales* 2023). Those cases which proceed before court tend to be disposed of during one hearing or a short trial (*Justice Data* 2023) and in 52 per cent of cases, at least one party is unrepresented (*Civil Justice Statistics Quarterly: October to December 2022* 2023). The pre-court stages differ depending on whether the cases are assigned a small claims, fast track or multi-track procedure but would typically include a directions questionnaire which helps courts determine the most appropriate track and, subsequently, request documents from the relevant pre-trial checklist (e.g. disclosures, expert reports, witness statements – *CPR Rules and Directions*). Small claims proceedings are geared towards SRLs, and so the expectation is that they are manageable for lay court users. But there are no recent statistics or research reports on how SRLs are coping with the process and what their success rates are or the challenges they are experiencing (cf. previous studies, such as Moorhead and Sefton 2005; Moorhead 2007; Lewis 2007).

The observed sample of ten money-related (small claims) hearings showed that language and communication played a significant role in creating, framing and resolving small claims disputes. As all the evidence is typically heard within the same hearing (unless the initial hearing is adjourned for lack of disclosures or incomplete procedural steps), from the perspective of narrativisation, these hearings present an opportunity to deliver the macro narrative in its entirety. However, there is still the separation into several narrativisation-related stages within the hearing: the evidentiary stage, submissions, judgement on substantial matters, costs justification (whether the winning party's costs should be covered by the losing party), and judgement on costs. Across these hearing or trial stages, there are several narrativisation threads: the narrative of dispute onset (e.g. whether the agreement or contractual conditions were established), narrative of dispute resolution (whether the parties attempted to resolve the dispute or settle it), parties' case narratives (the evidence presented and submissions made by the parties), parties' cost narratives (reasoning for who should cover the court fees and legal costs) and, potentially, the narrative of the judicial decision-making (if the previous judicial decisions on, for instance, instructing an expert witness impact the case narrative).

Similar to the findings made in the ethnographic studies by O'Barr and Conley (O'Barr and Conley 1985, 1991; Conley and O'Barr 1988), the observations conducted for this study showed that the narratives presented by court users were very different in their structure and content focus from those expected by the judiciary and required by courts and the legal system. What stood out in the observations was that the differences were mainly due to the fact that the internal structure of narratives did not observe the key procedural aspects, such as the distinction between evidence and submissions (see the discussion of the same issue in relation to the child-related proceedings). For instance, in case 28, when the court user started to explain what the evidence showed (while passing evidential images and documents to the judge) the judge interrupted them by saying 'first evidence, then submissions'. It is not clear whether this was sufficient as an explanation, but for the remainder of the hearing, the judge supported the party by eliciting the required information (e.g. 'Do you have any other evidence?', 'Do you want to ask the other party anything?').

In another small claims hearing (case 30), the submissions stage became very chaotic when an SRL respondent party was asked to cross-examine the SRL claimants, a building company which carried out repairs for them. Conducting cross-examination is a notoriously difficult discursive task for any lay court user as it requires a complex set of discursive competencies for narrating the story through questions (cf. Tkacukova 2010; Yeung and Leung 2019; Trinder et al. 2014; Lewis 2007; Moorhead and Sefton 2005; McKeever et al. 2018). When cross-examining, the respondent kept explaining what happened rather than asking questions, which meant that the judge had to interrupt several times and encourage the respondent to introduce questions: 'You are telling me, but you need to ask questions', 'Do you want to challenge?', 'Is there a question there?', 'Isn't it right that [rephrasing the defendant's sentence]', 'Isn't it right that you told me (prompting the defendant to change the sentence into a questions with this initiation)?', 'Make it into a question', 'Isn't it correct that (prompting the defendant to change the sentence into a questions with this initiation)'. After twenty minutes of the SRL's unsuccessful attempt at cross-examination, the judge decided to change the strategy and ask the questions on their own: 'I'll ask the questions.' Moving away from a strictly adversarial approach (similar to case 28 already discussed) allowed the judge to elicit the narrative of the dispute onset ('Judge: Do you accept they offered to do extra work? / Claimant: Yes') and case narratives:

> Judge: Now tell me why I should decide in your favour.
> The respondent: They knew the look I wanted.
> The claimant: It is regrettable. We have many customers. We don't have a crystal ball, we advise many customers within the budget, but don't go and tell them what to do. (. . .) [The respondent] just rejected.

This helped the judge establish that there was 'no breach of the consumer regulation' and rule in favour of the claimant, with the defendant having to pay the sum owed to the claimant and court fees. Without the judge performing a more active role in eliciting the evidence and the narratives, it would have been very challenging to determine the relevance of substantive matters. The fact that SRLs are expected to conduct cross-examination illustrates that the small claims process does not fully acknowledge the challenges of legal participation for lay court users.

Unfortunately, SRL parties are procedurally disadvantaged in other ways as well. For instance, instructing experts is a particularly complex task from the procedural and discursive perspectives. From the procedural point of view, the instructions need to fulfil the practice directions and procedural requirements (*CPR*, Part 35 on experts and assessors). From the discursive point of view, expert witnesses owe a duty to the court, which restricts the parties' options when framing the questions for expert witnesses and attempting to limit the scope of the report to their benefit. In case 36, the judge warns an SRL in a semi-represented case about instructing experts:

> It doesn't mean an expert will support [your view]. It's extraordinary on the part of the expert to do so – what do you think he'll be doing? (. . .) Experts are brazen about their views. They are law unto themselves. The court is allowing you to get a joint expert, so spend your money wisely. CPR tells us how to instruct an expert.

While in the previously discussed case, the judiciary eventually supported SRLs with the discursive task of cross-examining witnesses, here the judge does not step outside of the adversarial role, and the discursively challenging task of instructing an expert witness is left for a solicitor for the other party and the SRL to agree on. The risk is that the represented party can gain an advantageous position through framing of the instructions. Another aspect to note is that the judge in this case, similar to other judges in small claims cases, relied on the jargon and abbreviations (e.g. 'CPR' for Civil Procedure Rules, without referring to the relevant Part 35 of the CPR provision in case 36, 'submissions' from the previously discussed case 28).

The references to CPR were repeatedly made by several judges as a way of explaining what is expected from witness statements and the requirements for the provision of evidence. In case 38, the judge referred to specific sections of the practice directions: 'Have a look at these provisions [Part 16 CPR, 16.2, 16.4].' The SRL did not appear to take notes and even if they were to find the relevant part of the CPR, the rules only list the genres and their brief content. The intended audience of the procedure rules is legal professionals and the communicative aim of the rules is to provide a checklist of the documents and pre-court procedural steps to be followed (as shown in the following example). SRLs, irrespective of their educational or professional background, are unlikely to have discursive competence to construct effective statements without the support (cf. Trinder et al. 2014) and exemplification of discursive strategies (cf. Grieshofer 2023a):

Contents of the particulars of claim 16.4
(1) Particulars of claim must include –
    (a) a concise statement of the facts on which the claimant relies;
    (b) if the claimant is seeking interest, a statement to that effect and the details set out in paragraph (2);
    (c) if the claimant is seeking aggravated damages (GL) or exemplary damages(GL), a statement to that effect and the grounds for claiming them;
    (d) if the claimant is seeking provisional damages, a statement to that effect and the grounds for claiming them; and
    (e) such other matters as may be set out in a practice direction.
(2) If the claimant is seeking interest they must –
    (a) state whether they are doing so –
        (i) under the terms of a contract;
        (ii) under an enactment and, if so, which; or
        (iii) on some other basis and, if so, what that basis is; and

   (b) if the claim is for a specified amount of money, state –
        (i) the percentage rate at which interest is claimed;
       (ii) the date from which it is claimed;
     (iii) the date to which it is calculated, which must not be later than the date on which the claim form is issued;
     (iv) the total amount of interest claimed to the date of calculation; and
      (v) the daily rate at which interest accrues after that date.
         (Part 22 requires particulars of claim to be verified by a statement of truth).

(Civil Procedure Rules)

Apart from the overreliance on terminology and referring to CPR as the main source of information, the judiciary were very effective in explaining the key procedural and legal aspects as well as ensuring that SRLs had an opportunity to project their voices. For instance, at the beginning of one hearing, the judge provided a clear explanation of the burden of proof, how the interaction would work and what will happen in the end:

> I am going to decide this case on the balance of probabilities [explains this equates to 51% certainty]. When I am talking to one person, I need everyone else to be quiet. But I'll give you an opportunity to speak. At the end of the case, whoever loses you can ask me for a permission to appeal, but ask me before you leave. I need to feel you have a chance, so more than 51% (case 29).

Court users were also supported with developing their legal arguments in situations when they lacked legal understanding or procedural awareness. In case 9, the SRL applicant was allowed to pursue their claim, despite the fact that the proceedings were initiated several years after the permissible time frame according to the Limitation Act 1980. Upon the discussion of the time frame, the judge made it clear what the law states: 'You are alleging they were negligent. You are aware there is only a six years' window, but extra provision is for three years', and then enquiring how the SRL could support their argument for the delayed initiation of the proceedings: 'Judge: What legislative provision? / SRL: I don't know, but I complained on their website because it took long to get a formal response. If I had it sooner, I would have instigated the proceedings sooner.' This was sufficient for the SRL to be permitted to proceed with the claim (the actual hearing was adjourned for a later period).

    In another hearing (case 33), the judge presiding over a semi-represented bankruptcy case admonished the solicitor representing the applicants for bringing several statutory demand claims in different county courts across the country against the same SRL respondent. Once the SRL mentioned the applicants' conduct and the number of legal cases they were facing, the judge reacted by saying: 'I am a little concerned about machine gunning of statutory demands. (. . .) This is the abuse of process of statutory demands.' The moment the solicitor attempted to justify the claimants' legal strategy, the judge interrupted by saying: 'Stop relying on statutory demands and focus on the real issues.' By unifying all the legal claims into one, the judge stepped outside of their discursive role defined by the adversarial approach but at the same time acted in accordance with professional ethics (cf. Boettcher 2014).

In the previously mentioned case (case 36), where the SRL respondent wanted to instruct an expert witness, the judge made it clear that court time is valuable by interrupting the SRL and a solicitor representing the applicant. This created the condition in which voice projection would theoretically be difficult, but in practice the judge inferred what the evidence was saying, without the parties explicitly expressing their arguments. When the judge created an opportunity for voice projection ('Anything else you might want me to take into account?'), the SRL managed to provide an email as evidence of their attempt to resolve the case prior to court:

> I have not done anything wrong. I only asked questions and proposed options to move forward, only written polite emails and I shouldn't be liable for the solicitor costs. [The Applicant] wasn't waiting for my response and [the Applicant] was ready to take it to court.

This prompted the judge to interrupt the SRL and address both parties: 'I have to cut you short. When I see an email like this – an offer, and you [solicitor] are saying you want the time in court – court time is a valuable resource and shouldn't be used to express your grievances.' Further interaction was very brief, goal-oriented and controlled by the judge:

> SRL Respondent: Can I add to that?
> Judge: No, I don't want any submissions on that. So no costs on legal fees for the time being.
> Solicitor for Applicant: May I address you?
> Judge: No, you shouldn't have come to court.
> (. . .)
> Solicitor: If we don't agree . . .
> Judge: Clarify and agree.

Similar to the previously mentioned cases (9 and 33), the SRL's voice projection is supported by the judiciary who lower their expectations as to the discursive competence and proceed with the decisions based on partial narratives, in which legal relevance is not always clearly presented by the parties but can be deducted from the evidence presented.

It is also important to note that the judgements delivered by the judiciary in small claims proceedings played an important role for informational justice. What stood out is that despite the informal manner of the proceedings which were held in small judiciary offices, the delivery of judgement was the only part with a strong function of a performative ritual (cf. Heffer 2013). The multi-audience nature of the judgements was apparent from the functions the judges performed: delivering the judgement to the parties, summarising the substantive issues in the case for the parties and potentially an appeals court, explaining the decision-making process for the benefit of the parties and potential appeal judges, offering an element of public legal education for the parties and the wider public by explaining the relevant law and record keeping for court purposes by audio-recording their judgement. For instance, in case 18 in relation to the parking charges an SRL defendant did not pay (arguing they could not see the parking signs), the judgement fulfils several functions: 'The position on the law is quite clear and there are enough signs. Whilst I sympathise with his position, [respondent] needs to pay [monetary sum] fine'; and later in relation to the costs claim, the judge's ruling is: 'The claimant applies for [monetary sum] fixed costs. The defendant resists due to not enough steps were taken to notify [defendant]. I entirely accept [pronoun for respondent] point, however [respondent] provided an email as the main contact (. . .). I have sympathy for the situation, but the claimant is entitled to recover fixed costs.' The empathy repeatedly expressed by the judge plays an important role in communicating that the respondent's voice was heard, even though the arguments were not strong enough from the legal perspective. Similarly, in another semi-represented parking ticket hearing (case 28), the judgement also fulfils several functions and considers multiple audiences:

> The claimant's case is that originally judgement in default was entered. I've heard the witness statement from the defendant. The issue with ([signage] . . .). The claimant relies on the claimant's witness statement. [The claimant] is not in court, but it is admissible. The weight I can attach to this is less than if [the claimant] had attended. But the burden of proof with the claimant is on the balance of probabilities, so that means more likely than not. It is important to keep signage as (. . .) contract. According to the witness statement of the claimant, the signage is exhibited in photographs, but it is difficult to work out the legend on the map. Bearing in mind this evidence and that it is not challenged by the defendant, I am persuaded on the balance of probabilities that the signage is appropriate. The next issue is who the driver was (. . .) (looking at evidence). Because up to now there has been no mention of who the driver was, I am persuaded that the defendant was the driver. The claimant has proved the case and is to get [monetary sum] fixed cost.

Reflecting on the outcome after the hearings, both respondents felt it was a lot of money (given it was for a parking fee) but did not feel that the decision-making process was unfair as the judge explained the rationale behind the decision process.

Overall, the observations showed that there was sufficient support offered from the judiciary during the hearings (see also Tkacukova 2015). The support took different shapes but ultimately ensured that the parties' voices (irrespective of whether they were represented or not) could be projected and their arguments could be considered. One of the most effective strategies used by the judiciary was to reframe and summarise the parties' narrativisation threads in order to establish common ground and accelerate the process. The explanation provided was usually embedded in the elicitation strategies, instructions on further steps or judgement summaries, and was mainly presented using everyday language. On occasion, the judiciary used legal and procedural terms and references which would typically be outside of the lay parties' semantic field and discursive competence. But the main issues were linked to the fact that the pre-court procedural stages and institutional overreliance on complex genres without much discursive support created even more serious issues with respect to process control and informational justice, which essentially positioned lay court users as outsiders and discursively disadvantaged them (e.g. referring to CRP is not sufficient as it does not address SRLs' needs). The observations also showed that with some of the discursive aspects, such as cross-examination, the challenges could be alleviated if the judge stepped in and disregarded the fully adversarial mode of adjudication, but the same strategy cannot be easily adopted in cases where the procedural steps happen mainly out of court (e.g. provision of an expert witness report for out-of-court negotiations). Exploring discursive practices as a continuum throughout the pre-court court stages is instrumental for identifying gaps in the suitability of the small claims processes and procedures for lay court users.

9 Concluding Thoughts and Future Directions

The Element contributes to the interdisciplinary research agenda shared across courtroom discourse studies, language and law studies, socio-legal studies, administrative and public law, while also establishing a discursive framework to support legal practice, procedure rule committees and courts and tribunals services. From the research perspective, the Element proposes several conceptual developments: introducing the discourse of legal proceedings as a term highlighting the continuity between pre-court and court stages; establishing a methodological framework for exploring discursive practices embedded in out-of-court procedural stages and court hearings; consolidating an interdisciplinary approach to ethnographic methods in court research; contextualising discursive practices as part of court processes and procedures; and interlinking theoretical frameworks of discursive practices, legal participation and procedural justice.

From the perspective of legal practice, the Element argues that in order to reinforce procedural justice tenets, it is crucial to consider the impact of practice directions, procedure rules and adjudicative approaches on discursive practices and voice projection opportunities for court users. In the first instance, this includes a unified approach to the provision of pre-court legal and procedural information which is tailored to lay court users' needs, simplification of pre-court elicitation strategies and genres and provision of support for narrativisation and argument construction. On the broader institutional and professional levels, it is important to raise the awareness of legal professionals and justice reformers of (1) the significant role legal–lay communication plays in determining the substantive aspects of the proceedings and strategies which can support tailored elicitation of court users' narratives, (2) the urgent need to adjust adversarialism and its procedural complexity to consolidate and streamline narrativisation requirements throughout the proceedings and (3) the imperative to incorporate the needs of lay court users in the design of procedure rules (e.g. to ensure they can be supported in instructing an expert witness) and the content of procedure rules (e.g. creating a practical guide to the rules which are most relevant for SRLs). As the Element illustrates that exploring discursive practices can contribute to the discussion of procedural aspects of legal proceedings and systemic issues in the justice system, the hope is that court and tribunal services will see the relevance of the linguistic input into the design of texts (court forms, online applications, guidance documents, procedure rules) as well as pre-court and court procedures (what, how and when the information is elicited from the parties).

By exploring three types of most common proceedings heard in family and county courts, the Element shows some variability within the discursive practices across the private family proceedings and small claims hearings. This points to the fact that substantive law and corresponding court procedures impact elicitation and narrativisation practices throughout the proceedings; similarly, the judiciary's role within different types of proceedings impacts voice projection opportunities during hearings. Child-related proceedings are paradoxically very restrictive when it comes to opportunities for court users to project their voices and share their stories. Routine and irretrievable muting of the children and parents' voices happens due to poor language data management (i.e. Cafcass not audio-recording the interviews, which leads to potential complications with reporting and non-existent quality assurance measures for interviewing and reporting processes) and due to the postponement of direct narration opportunities to the final hearing (i.e. approximately a year after the proceedings start). The study presented here is not the first to point to the fact that court users' voices are muted in family proceedings; in fact, the findings echo the concerns expressed in much of the current socio-legal research showing that families are not heard in courts across jurisdictions internationally (cf. Hunter et al. 2020). Drawing on the theoretical framework of discursive practices and linguistically driven ethnography, this study was able to go beyond the general observation: the Element identifies the stages at which the voices are muted as well as illustrates how court procedures impact voice projection opportunities throughout the proceedings. The delay in eliciting the narratives in court settings, compounded by the overall lack of opportunities for narratives to be elicited in the supportive and well-structured interactive format, means that parties find themselves in the position when they can only observe what happens to their original (often restricted) stories as they take shape through expert-led and expert-framed genres and move away from the original meaning. Furthermore, due to the institutional narrative of promoting out-of-court settlement and incorporating adjudicative genres in pre-court stages, most of the parties do not reach the final hearing stage, which is the stage which allocates the first opportunity to parties to share at least some aspects of the narrative in the interactive format. Although from the case management point of view, resolving the dispute without the need for the final hearing or prolonged proceedings is undoubtedly beneficial, it is the quantity and structure of initial procedural stages and the delay in the elicitation of parties' narratives that create multiple barriers for families. Those court users who do not reach the final hearing thus experience procedural barriers at the beginning of the proceedings but later miss an opportunity to share their stories in court before the judge or have their arguments considered by the judge (and instead have to simply read a Cafcass report which provides recommendations). The lack of these experiences undeniably impacts the court users' perceptions of procedural justice (Grieshofer 2023b) and the degree to which they accept unfavourable outcomes (cf. Lens 2016; Bendall 2020).

This aspect is, however, managed more efficiently during financial remedy proceedings: court procedures in financial remedy cases include a resolution hearing before parties can proceed to the final hearing. The communicative aim of the resolution hearing is for the judiciary to evaluate the parties' evidence and narratives and discuss possible solutions. On the one hand, this role of the judiciary is crucial in saving the court's time and encouraging informed negotiations between the parties. And, on the one hand, this type of hearing provides an opportunity for parties to project their voices in response to specific questions and have their arguments and narratives considered. As a result, despite the inherent adversarialism of the proceedings, the judiciary retain an active role in eliciting the evidence and providing support with framing financial needs narratives. The judicial discourse in observed hearings was often exemplary in addressing the needs of lay court users: short and clear questions created a cognitive structure for coherent elicitation of information, the summaries of arguments and evaluation of strengths and weaknesses of each party's case provided sufficient clarity about judicial decision-making principles tailored to individual cases. But before the parties reach the stage of the resolution hearing, there are many discursively complex court forms they are required to complete, often without clear instructions or explanations of relevant concepts. Informational justice in pre-court stages is thus the weakest part on the court users' journey to accessing procedural justice in financial remedy proceedings. As the main evidence is collected via two main forms, investing resources into the clarity of the forms would undoubtedly further improve discursive practices in private family courts.

The money-related civil claims present slightly different challenges: challenges in relation to communication around the context of the proceedings (i.e. the narrative of dispute onset is defined through the reconstruction of communication in relation to the agreement, the narrative of dispute resolution and costs narrative are defined through evidencing communication in relation to the parties' attempts to settle the case and reduce the costs) and case narrativisation (the presentation of evidence and submissions). The latter is further complicated by the procedure rules which were designed for fully represented cases and thus do not fully take into account SRLs' needs (e.g. challenges when cross-examining a witness, instructing an expert witness), despite the small claims track being perceived as suitable for lay court users. In the observed hearings, the judiciary followed the pre-defined procedures even when these complicated the interaction and did not lead to establishing substantive matters in the case. But once the judiciary stepped outside of the adversarial approach and took a more active role in eliciting submissions, they could establish a clear and coherent elicitation strategy and address lay narrativisation needs. The main barrier for procedural justice in small claims cases is the procedural complexity during pre-court and court stages, resembling the challenges during the child-related proceedings and financial remedy proceedings (though this applies mainly to pre-court stages). More careful consideration needs to be given to court processes and procedures in semi-represented and fully unrepresented cases, especially in cases where SRLs are envisaged as the main users of the proceedings.

To reflect on the overall systemic issues observed in the three types of proceedings, the current form of adversarialism as practised in family and county courts is somewhat misplaced due to the procedural focus and complex requirements imposed on court users (cf. Hunter et al. 2020; Grieshofer 2023b). While in court the judiciary tend to mitigate the challenges of procedural complexity and create opportunities for court users to be heard, the pre-court stages present multiple difficulties for many represented and unrepresented parties as they have to present their narratives in multiple genres mostly unfamiliar to them, and sometimes even witness how their narratives are reinterpreted and reframed without an opportunity to correct them. Presenting the narratives or at least narrativisation threads in interaction with the judiciary is the most effective way for court users to have their voices heard, but this is only possible in the final hearings or pre-final hearings as the principle of orality yields to procedural complexity (Lazer 2021). Despite the fact that adversarial approach is in theory best suited for encouraging parties to project their voices (Ainsworth 2015), its current implementation overburdens court users who then need to be supported by the judiciary to clarify their arguments. The solutions proposed here are to simplify the procedural steps court users need to take, ensure court users have an opportunity to express their voices much earlier in the proceedings, establish clear rules around language data management and recording and reporting on court users' narratives, and introduce resolution hearings or other opportunities for the parties to understand the judicial decision-making principles applicable to their cases (Holt and Thomson 2023).

The study indicates several directions in which further research and court reform programmes could develop. It is important to adopt an interdisciplinary approach and investigate how to improve the provision of legal and procedural information, simplify the elicitation techniques in pre-court stages and reduce the number of genres court users need to be submitting without diminishing the quality of pre-court disclosures or interfering with legal requirements for a fair process. Similarly, discursive processes in online courts and remote hearings (telephone and online hearings) need to be explored from the point of view of procedural justice, that is, beyond the currently applied, often superficial user experience criteria (cf. *HMCTS Reform: Achievements, Challenges and Next Steps* 2023). It is also imperative to conduct further research on the overview of discursive practices in other types of proceedings, especially those where lay court users or vulnerable participants play a crucial role (e.g. proceedings in employment tribunals, immigration tribunals, special educational needs and disability tribunals, social security and child support tribunals, bankruptcy cases, public family cases, other civil and criminal cases).

Procedural justice and legal participation cannot be achieved without ensuring that the established discursive practices can accommodate legal–lay discursive differences. The role of linguistic input is important not only for identifying and addressing communicative issues but also for ensuring procedure rules and practice directions are designed in accordance with linguistic principles which are at the core of elicitation and narrativisation practices. As an inherent part of procedural justice, discursive practices help define the quality of the case-level communication as well as contribute to the institutional image of courts and tribunals and the citizens' trust in the justice system (cf. Jackson et al. 2012).

Appendix: Court Observations Template

Participants (underline if applies) Claimant/Applicant – SRL/represented by solicitor/barrister Respondent – SRL/represented by solicitor/barrister Judiciary – Judge/district judge/magistrates (number) Legal adviser Other – social services, Cafcass officer Other – expert witness Other –	Abbreviations for participants For example, C + S (claimant represented by a solicitor)

Case introduction/summary stage

Speakers	Topics covered, topics agreed/not agreed	Interaction pattern (e.g. SRL > DJ, i.e. SRL addressing district judge)

Main part (post-introduction stage)

Speakers	Topics initiated, elicitation/narrativisation/explanation strategies	Interaction pattern

Outcome of the hearing and directions/orders made

Parties who expressed the wish for a specific direction/order	Directions/orders, instructions	Responsibilities

Reflections

References

Adler, M. (2012). The Plain language movement. In P. Tiersma and L. Solan, eds., *The Oxford Handbook of Language and Law*. Oxford: Oxford University Press, pp. 67–83.

Ainsworth, J. (2015). Legal discourse and legal narratives. *Language and Law/ Linguagem e Direito*, 2(1), 1–11.

Assy, R. (2011). Can the law speak directly to its subjects? The limitation of plain language. *Journal of Law and Society*, 383, 376–404.

Assy, R. (2015). *Injustice in Person: The Right to Self-representation*. Oxford: Oxford University Press.

Azuelos-Atias, S. (2011). On the incoherence of legal language to the general public. *International Journal for the Semiotics of Law*, 24(1), 41–59.

Baffy, M. & Marsters, A. (2015). The constructed voice in courtroom cross-examination. *International Journal of Speech, Language & the Law*, 22(2), 143–165.

Bednarek, G. (2014). *Polish vs. American Courtroom Discourse: Inquisitorial and Adversarial Procedures of Witness Examination in Criminal Trials*. London: Palgrave.

Bendall, C. (2020). Should we welcome an end to the 'blame game'? Reflecting on experiences of civil partnership dissolution. *Journal of Divorce & Remarriage*, 61(5), 344–365.

Bhatia, V. K. (2004). *Worlds of Written Discourse*. New York: Continuum.

Bhatia, V. K. (2006). Discursive practices in disciplinary and professional contexts. *Linguistics and the Human Sciences*, 2(1), 5–28.

Bhatia, V. K. & Bhatia, A. (2011). Legal discourse across cultures and socio-pragmatic contexts. *World Englishes*, 30(4), 481–495.

Black, R., Cleary, A. & Culworth, W. (eds.). (2014). *The Family Court Practice*. Family Law. LexisNexis.

Block, M. K. & Parker, J. S. (2004). Decision making in the absence of successful fact finding: Theory and experimental evidence on adversarial versus inquisitorial systems of adjudication. *International Review of Law and Economics*, 24(1), 89–105.

Boettcher, J., Cavanagh, G. & Xu, M. (2014). Ethical issues that arise in bankruptcy. *Business and Society Review*, 119(4), 473–496.

Boréus, K. (2006). Discursive discrimination: A typology. *European Journal of Social Theory*, 9(3), 405–424.

Braun, S. & Taylor, J. L. (2012). *Videoconference and Remote Interpreting in Criminal Proceedings.* Antwerp and Cambridge: Intersentia.

Carbaugh, D. (1989). The critical voice in ethnography of communication research. *Research on Language & Social Interaction*, 23(1–4), 261–281.

Cheng, E. K. & Nunn, G. (2019). Beyond the witness: Bringing process perspective to modern evidence law. *Texas Law Review*, 97(6), 1077–1124.

Conley, J. M. & O'Barr, W. M. (1988). Fundamentals of jurisprudence: An ethnography of judicial decision making in informal courts. *North Carolina Law Review*, 66(3), 467–508.

Conley, J. M. & O'Barr, W. M. (1990). *Rules versus Relationships: The Ethnography of Legal Discourse.* Chicago: University of Chicago Press.

Conley, J. M. & O'Barr, W. M. (1998). *Just Words: Law, Language, and Power.* Chicago: University of Chicago.

Cooper, P. & Mattison, M. (2021). *Witness Statements for the Employment Tribunal in England and Wales: What are the Issues?* London: Institute for Crime and Justice Policy Research.

Cotterill, J. (ed.) (2002). *Language in the Legal Process.* Basingstoke: Palgrave Macmillan.

Cotterill, J. (2003). *Language and Power in Court: A Linguistic Analysis of the OJ Simpson trial.* London: Palgrave.

Coulthard, M. & Johnson, A. (2007). *Introducing Forensic Linguistics: Language in Evidence.* New York: Routledge.

Coulthard, M., May, A. & Sousa-Silva, R. (eds.) (2021, 2nd ed.). *The Routledge Handbook of Forensic Linguistics.* London and New York: Routledge.

Crisp, J., Hunter, R. & Hitchings, E. (2022). Domestic abuse in financial remedy cases. *Financial Remedies Journal*, 2, 123–126.

Cusworth, L., Bedston, S., Alrouh, B. et al. (2021). *Uncovering Private Family Law: Who's Coming to Court in England?* London: Nuffield Family Justice Observatory.

Danet, B., Hoffman, K., Kermish, N., Rafn, J. & Stayman, D. (1980). An ethnography of questioning in the courtroom. In R. W. Shuy and A. Shnukal, eds., *Language Use and the Uses of Language.* Washington, DC: Georgetown University Press, pp. 171–179.

Davies, B. L. (2013). Travelling texts: The legal-lay interface in the highway code. In C. Heffer, F. Rock and J. Conley, eds., *Legal-Lay Communication: Textual Travels in the Law.* Oxford: Oxford University Press, pp. 266–287.

Devine, L. (2015). Considering social work assessment of families. *Journal of Social Welfare and Family Law*, 37(1), 70–83.

D'hondt, S. (2021). Why being there mattered: Staged transparency at the International Criminal Court. *Journal of Pragmatics*, 183, 168–178.

D'hondt, S. & May, A. (2022). Engaging with the field while studying language in the legal process: Windows of engagement and normative moorings. *Journal of Pragmatics*, 199, 1–5.

Doak, J., Jackson, J., Saunders, C. et al. (2021). *Cross-examination in Criminal Trials Towards a Revolution in Best Practice? A Report for the Nuffield Foundation.* http://irep.ntu.ac.uk/id/eprint/44965/1/1496788_Doak.pdf.

Dumas, B. K. (2002). Reasonable doubt about reasonable doubt: Assessing jury instruction adequacy in a capital case. In J. Cotterill, ed., *Language in the Legal Process*. London: Palgrave Macmillan, pp. 241–259.

Eades, D. (1996). Verbatim courtroom transcripts and discourse analysis. In H. Kniffka, ed., *Recent Developments in Forensic Linguistics*. Frankfurt: Peter Lang, pp. 241–254.

Eades, S. (2010). *Sociolinguistics and the Legal Process*. Bristol: Multilingual Matters.

Ehrlich, S. (2010). Courtroom discourse. In R. Wodak, B. Johnstone and E. Kerswill, eds., *The SAGE Handbook of Sociolinguistic*. London: Sage, pp. 361–375.

Ehrlich, S. (2010). The discourse of rape trials. In M. Coulthard and A. May, eds., *The Routledge Handbook of Forensic Linguistics*. London and New York: Routledge, pp. 265–281.

Ejimabo, N. O. (2015). The effective research process: Unlocking the advantages of ethnographic strategies in the qualitative research methods. *European Scientific Journal*, 11(23), 356–383.

Ellison, L. (2001). The mosaic art? Cross-examination and the vulnerable witness. *Legal Studies*, 21(3), 353–375.

Firestone, G. & Weinstein, J. (2004). In the best interests of children: A proposal to transform the adversarial system. *Family Court Review*, 42(2), 203–215.

Flood, J. (2005). Socio-legal ethnography. In R. Banakar and M. Travers, eds., *Theory and Method in Socio-Legal Research*. Portand: Hart, pp. 33–48.

Fraser, H. (2003). Issues in transcription: Factors affecting the reliability of transcripts as evidence in legal cases. *Forensic Linguistics*, 10(2), 203–226.

Freiberg, A. (2011). Post-adversarial and post-inquisitorial justice: Transcending traditional penological paradigms. *European Journal of Criminology*, 8(1), 82–101.

Gales, T. & Wing, D. (2022). Forensic linguistic data and resources. Accessed on 30 March 2023. www.forensicling.com/.

Genn, H. (1999). *Paths to Justice: What People Do and Think about Going to Law*. Oxford: Hart.

Gibb, R. (2019). Communicative practices and contexts of interaction in the refugee status determination process in France. In N. Gill and A. Good, eds.,

Asylum Determination in Europe: Ethnographic Perspectives. Cham, Switzerland: Palgrave Macmillan, pp. 155–174.

Gibbons, J. (2003). *Forensic Linguistics: An Introduction to Language in the Legal System*. London: Blackwell.

Gibbons, J. (ed.) (2014). *Language and the Law*. London: Routledge.

Gracean, J. M. (2014). Self-represented litigants, the courts, and the legal profession: Myths and realities. *Family Court Review*, 662–669. https://doi.org/10.1111/fcre.12118.

Grant, T. (2010). Forensic linguistics – advancing justice. In K. Richards and J. Uglow, eds., *The New Optimist: Scientists View Tomorrow's World & What it Means to Us*. Birmingham: Linus, pp. 217–221.

Gray, P. R. (2010). The expert witness problem. *International Journal of Speech, Language & the Law*, 17(2), 201–209.

Grieshofer, T. (2022a). Remote interpreting in immigration tribunals. *International Journal for the Semiotics of Law*, 36, 767–788. https://doi.org/10.1007/s11196-022-09908-3.

Grieshofer, T. (2022b). The importance of being heard: Stories of unrepresented litigants in small claims cases and private family proceedings. *Language and Law – Linguagem e Direito*, 9(1), 1–19. https://ojs.letras.up.pt/index.php/LLLD/article/view/12827.

Grieshofer, T. (2022c). Lay advisers in family law settings: The role and quality of advice provided on social media. *Social & Legal Studies*, 31(6), 941–960. https://doi.org/10.1177/09646639221090132

Grieshofer, T. (2023a). Court forms as part of online courts: Elicitation and communication in the early stages of legal proceedings. *International Journal for the Semiotics of Law*, 36, 1843–1881. https://doi.org/10.1007/s11196-023-09993-y.

Grieshofer, T. (2023b). Reimagining communication and elicitation strategies in private family proceedings. *Journal of Social Welfare and Family Law*, 45(1), 41–61. https://doi.org/10.1080/09649069.2023.2175546.

Grieshofer, T., Gee, M. & Morton, R. (2021). The journey to comprehensibility: Court forms as the first barrier to accessing justice. *International Journal for the Semiotics of Law*, 35, 1733–1759. https://doi.org/10.1007/s11196-021-09870-6.

Hans, V. P. (2003). Lay participation in legal decision making. *Law & Policy*, 25(2), 83–92.

Harris, S. (1984). Questions as a mode of control in Magistrates' courts. *International Journal of the Sociology of Language*, 49, 5–27.

Harris, S. (2005). Telling stories and giving evidence: The hybridisation of narrative and non-narrative modes of discourse in a sexual assault trial. In

J. Thornborrow and J. Coates, eds., *The Sociolinguistics of Narrative*. Amsterdam: Benjamins, pp. 215–237.

Harris, S. (2001). Fragmented narratives and multiple tellers: Witness and defendant accounts in trials. *Discourse Studies*, 3(1), 53–74.

Haworth, K. (2013). Audience design in the police interview: The interactional and judicial consequences of audience orientation. *Language in Society*, 42(1), 45–69.

Haworth, K. (2018). Tapes, transcripts and trials: The routine contamination of police interview evidence. *The International Journal of Evidence & Proof*, 22(4), 428–450.

Heffer, C., Rock, F. & Conley, J. (eds.). (2013). *Legal-Lay Communication: Textual Travels in the Law*. Oxford: Oxford University Press.

Heffer, C. (2013). Communication and magic: Authorized voice, legal-linguistic habitus, and the recontextualization of "Beyond Reasonable Doubt." In C. Heffer, F. Rock and J. Conley, eds., *Legal-Lay Communication: Textual Travels in the Law*. Oxford: Oxford University Press, pp. 206–225.

Heffer, C. (2007). The language of conviction and the convictions of certainty: Is 'sure' an impossible standard of proof? *International Commentary on Evidence*, 5(1), art. 5.

Heffer, C. (2005). *The Language of Jury Trial: A Corpus-Aided Analysis of Legal-Lay Discourse*. Basingstoke: Springer.

Heffer, C. (2018). Suppression, silencing and failure to project: Ways of losing voice while using it. In R. Page, B. Busse and N. Norgaard, eds., *Rethinking Language, Text and Context: Interdisciplinary Research in Stylistics in Honour of Michael Toolan*. Routledge Studies in Rhetoric and Stylistics. London: Taylor & Francis, pp. 237–253.

Heenan, A. (2018). Causal and temporal connections in financial remedy cases: The meaning of marriage. *Child and Family Law Quarterly*, 30(1), 75–88.

Heritage, J. (2002). The limits of questioning: Negative interrogatives and hostile question content. *Journal of Pragmatics*, 34, 1427–1446.

Hitchcock, T., Shoemaker, R., Emsley, C., Howard, S. & McLaughlin, J. *The Old Bailey Proceedings Online, 1674–1913* (www.oldbaileyonline.org, version 7.0, 24 March 2012).

Hitchings, E. & Miles, J. (2016). Mediation, financial remedies, information provision and legal advice: The post-LASPO conundrum. *Journal of Social Welfare and Family Law*, 38(2), 175–195. https://doi.org/10.1080/09649069.2016.1156888.

Hitchings, E., Miles, J. & Woodward, H. (2014). Assembling the jigsaw puzzle: Understanding financial settlement on divorce. *Family Law*, 44, 309–318.

Hobbs, P. (2003). You must say it for him: Reformulating a witness testimony on cross-examination at trial. *Text & Talk*, 23(4), 477–511.

Holt, K. & Thomson, C. (2023). Autoethnography: A personal reflection on the work of the family bar in the North of England. *Journal of Social Welfare and Family Law*, 45(1), 62–80.

Hough, B. (2010). Self-represented litigants in family law: The response of California's courts. *The Circuit*. Paper 52. http://scholarship.law.berkeley.edu/clrcircuit/52.

Hunter, G. (2020). Policy and practice supporting lay participation. In J. Jacobson and P. Cooper, eds., *Participation in Courts and Tribunals: Concepts, Realities and Aspirations*. Bristol: Bristol University Press, pp. 19–64.

Hunter, R., Burton, M. & Trinder, L. (2020). *Assessing Risk of Harm to Children and Parents in Private Law Children Cases*. Ministry of Justice. Accessed on 30 March 2023. https://assets.publishing.service.gov.uk/government/uploads/system/uploads/attachment_data/file/895173/assessing-risk-harm-children-parents-pl-childrens-cases-report_.pdf.

Hunter, C., Nixon, J. & Blandy, S. (2008). Researching the judiciary: Exploring the invisible in judicial decision making. *Journal of Law and Society*, 35, 76–90.

Hunter, R., Anleu, S. R. & Mack, K. (2016). Judging in lower courts: Conventional, procedural, therapeutic and feminist approaches. *International Journal of Law in Context*, 12(3), 337–360.

Hunter, R. (2007). Close encounters of judicial kind: Hearing children's voices in family law proceedings. *Child and Family Law Quarterly*, 19(3), 283–303.

Hunter, R. (2005).Styles of judging: How magistrates deal with applications for intervention orders. *Alternative Law Journal*, 30(5), 231–246.

Hymes, D. (1962). The ethnography of speaking. In T. Gladwin and W. Sturtevant, eds., *Anthropology and Human Behavior*. Washington, DC: Anthropological Society of Washington, pp. 13–53.

Hymes, D. (1996). *Ethnography, Linguistics, Narrative Inequality: Toward an Understanding of Voice*. London: Taylor & Francis.

Jackson, J., Bradford, B., Hough, M., et al. (2012). Why do people comply with the law? Legitimacy and the influence of legal institutions. *British Journal of Criminology*, 52(6), 1051–1071.

Jacobson, J. (2020). Observed realities of participation. In J. Jacobson and P. Cooper, eds., *Participation in Courts and Tribunals*. Bristol: Bristol University Press, pp. 103–140.

Janney, R. W. (2002). Cotext as context: Vague answers in court. *Language and Communication*, 22, 457–475.

Jay, M. A., Byrom, N. & Forell, S. (2020). Innovative use of administrative data in legal research and practice. *International Journal of Population Data Science*, 5(5). https://doi.org/10.23889/ijpds.v5i5.1504.

Jean-Louis, S. (2021). I don't know what I'm doing: Using limited license legal technicians in family court to improve access to justice. *Family Court Review*, 59(3), 599–611.

Johnson, A. (2013). Embedding police interviews in the prosecution case in the Shipman trial. In Ch. Heffer, F. Rock and J. Conley, eds., *Legal-Lay Communication: Textual Travels in the Law*. Oxford: Oxford University Press, pp. 147–167.

Kaplow, L. (2011). Burden of proof. *Yale Law Journal*, 121, 738–859.

Kessler, A. D. (2004). Our inquisitorial tradition: Equity procedure, due process, and the search for an alternative to the adversarial. *Cornell Law Review*, 90, 1181, 1216–1217.

King, M., Freiberg, A., Batagol, B. & Hyams, R. (2014). *Non-adversarial Justice*. Sydney: Federation Press.

Komter, M. (2013). Travels of a suspect's statement. In Ch. Heffer, F. Rock and J. Conley, eds., *Legal-Lay Communication: Textual Travels in the Law*. Oxford: Oxford University Press, pp. 126–146.

Lande, J. (2003). Possibilities for collaborative law: Ethics and practice of lawyer disqualification and process control in a new model of lawyering. *Ohio State Law Journal*, 64, 1315–1384.

Laster, K. & Kornhauser, R. (2017). The rise of 'DIY' law: Implications for legal aid. In A. Flynn and J. Hodgson, eds., *Access to Justice and Legal Aid*. London: Bloomsbury, pp. 123–141.

Lazer, S. (2021). *The principle of orality: An analysis of the principles governing the prevalence of direct oral testimony in the English adversarial trial system and the impact of reforms to reduce its status*. Thesis (PhD). University of Huddersfield.

Lee, R. & Tkacukova, T. (2017). A study of litigants in person in Birmingham Civil Justice Centre. *CEPLER Working Paper Series 2*. http://epapers.bham.ac.uk/3014/1/cepler_working_paper_2_2017.pdf.

Lens, V. (2016). Against the grain: Therapeutic judging in a traditional family court. *Law & Social Inquiry*, 41(3), 701–718.

Lewis, P. (2007). Litigants in person and their difficulties in adducing evidence: A study of small claims in an English county court. *The International Journal of Evidence & Proof*, 11(1), 24–48.

Lind, E. A., Kanfer, R. & Earley, P. C. (1990). Voice, control, and procedural justice: Instrumental and noninstrumental concerns in fairness judgements. *Journal of Personality and Social psychology*, 59(5), 952–959.

Linder, D. O. (2023). *Famous Trials*. https://famous-trials.com/.

Lowndes, S. (2007). Barristers on trial: Comprehension and misapprehension in courtroom discourse. *International Journal of Speech, Language and the Law*, 14(2), 305–308.

Luchjenbroers, J. & Aldridge, M. (2008). Language and vulnerable witnesses across legal contexts: Introduction to the special issue. *Journal of English Linguistics*, 36(3), 191–194.

MacCoun, R. J. (2005). Voice, control, and belonging: The double-edged sword of procedural fairness. *Annual Review of Law and Social Science*, 1, 171–201.

Macfarlane, J. (2013). *The National Self-Represented Litigants Project: Identifying and Meeting the Needs of Self-Represented Litigants: Final Report*. British Columbia.

Macfarlane, J. (2005). Will changing the process change the outcome? The relationship between procedural and systemic change. *Louisiana Law Review*, 65, 1487–1508.

Maclean, M. (2010). Family mediation: Alternative or additional dispute resolution? *Journal of Social Welfare and Family Law*, 32(2), 105–106.

Maclean, M. & Eekelaar, J. (2019). *After the Act: Access to Family Justice after LASPO*. Oxford: Hart.

Maclean, M. & Eekelaar, J. (2016). *Lawyers and mediators: The brave new world of services for separating families*. Oxford and Portland: Hart.

MacLeod, N. & Haworth, K. (2017). Developing a linguistically informed approach to police interviewing. In R. Lawson and D. Sayers, eds., *Sociolinguistic Research: Application and Impact*. London and New York: Routledge, pp. 151–170.

Malsch, M. (2009). *Democracy in the Courts: Lay Participation in European Criminal Justice Systems*. London: Routledge.

Mant, J. (2022). *Litigants in Person and the Family Justice System*. Oxford: Hart.

Masson, L. (2012). 'I think I have strategies': Lawyers' approaches to parent engagement in care proceedings. *Child & Family Social Work*, 17(2), 202–211.

Matoesian, G. (2001). *Law and the Language of Identity: Discourse in the William Kennedy Smith Rape Trial*. Oxford: Oxford University Press.

McIntosh, J. E., Bryant, H. D. & Murray, K. (2008). Evidence of a different nature: The child-responsive and less adversarial initiatives of the family court of Australia. *Family Court Review*, 46(1), 125–136.

McKeever, G. (2020). Comparing courts and tribunals through the lens of legal participation. *Civil Justice Quarterly*, 39(3), 217–236.

McKeever, G., Royal-Dawson, L., Kirk, E. & McCord, J. (2018). *Litigants in Person in Northern Ireland: Barriers to Legal Participation*. Belfast: Ulster University.

Miles, J. K. & Hitchings, E. (2018). Financial remedy outcomes on divorce in England and Wales: Not a 'meal ticket for life'. *Australian Journal of Family Law*, 31(1 & 2), 43–80.

Moorhead, R. (2007). The passive arbiter: Litigants in person and the challenge to neutrality. *Social & Legal Studies*, 16(3), 405–424.

Moorhead, R. & Robinson, M. (2006). *A trouble shared – legal problems clusters in solicitors' and advice agencies*. Department for Constitutional Affairs Research Series, 8(6), https://orca.cardiff.ac.uk/id/eprint/5184/1/Moorhead_et_al_2006_A_Trouble_Shared.pdf.

Moorhead, R. L. & Sefton, M. (2005). *Litigants in person: Unrepresented litigants in first instance proceedings*. Department for Constitutional Affairs, 2(05), https://orca.cardiff.ac.uk/id/eprint/2956/1/1221.pdf

Newbury, P. & Johnson, A. (2006). Suspects' resistance to constraining and coercive questioning strategies in the police interview. *The International Journal of Speech, Language and the Law*, 13(2), 213–240.

Newman, C. (2010). *Expert Domestic Violence Risk Assessments in the Family Courts*. http://bds-research.com/Assessments/DVI/Research/domestic_violence_risk_assessment_in_family_court.pdf.

O'Barr, W. M. & Conley, J. M. (1991). Litigant satisfaction versus legal adequacy in small claims court narratives. In D. R. Papke, ed., *Narrative and the Legal Discourse: A Reader in Storytelling and the Law*. Liverpool: Deborah Charles, pp. 65–89.

O'Barr, W. M. (1982). *Linguistic Evidence: Language, Power, and Strategy in the Courtroom*. San Diego: Academic Press.

O'Barr, W. M. & Conley, J. M. (1985). Litigant satisfaction versus legal adequacy in small claim court narratives. *Law & Society Review*, 19(4), 661–702.

Pleasence, P. & Balmer, N. J. (2019). Justice & the capability to function in society. *Daedalus*, 148(1), 140–149.

Philips, S. (1987). On the use of Wh questions in American courtroom discourse: A Study of the relation between language form and language function. In D. Tannen and L. Kedar, eds., *Power through discourse*. Norwood, NJ: Ablex, pp. 83–112.

Reynolds, J. (2020). Investigating the language-culture nexus in refugee legal advice meetings. *Multilingua*, 39(4), 395–429.

Richardson, E., Sourdin, T. & Wallace, N. (2012). *Self-Represented Litigants: Literature Review*. https://ssrn.com/abstract=2713503 or http://dx.doi.org/10.2139/ssrn.2713503.

Richardson, E., Haworth, K. & Deamer, F. (2022). For the record: Questioning transcription processes in legal contexts. *Applied Linguistics*, 43(4), 677–697.

Rock, F., Heffer, C. & Conley, J. (2013). Textual travel in legal-lay communication. In C. Heffer, F. Rock and J. Conley, eds., *Legal-Lay Communication: Textual Travels in the Law*. Oxford:Oxford University Press, pp. 3–32.

Sacks, H., Schegloff, E. A. & Jefferson, G. (1974). A simplest systematics for the organization of turn-taking for conversation. *Language*, 50, 696–735.

Sandefur, R. (2015). Elements of professional expertise: Understanding relational and substantive expertise through lawyers' impact. *American Sociological Review*, 80(5), 909–933.

Sangasubana, N. (2011). How to conduct ethnographic research. *Qualitative Report*, 16(2), 567–573.

Sela, A. (2018). Can computers be fair: How automated and human-powered online dispute resolution affect procedural justice in mediation and arbitration. *Ohio State Journal on Dispute Resolution*, 33, 91–148.

Smith, L., Hitchings, E. & Sefton, M. (2017). A study of fee-charging McKenzie friends and their work in private family law cases. https://orca .cardiff.ac.uk/id/eprint/101919/1/A%20study%20of%20fee-charging% 20McKenzie%20Friends.pdf.

Solan, L. M. (2019). *The Language of Statutes: Laws and Their Interpretation*. Chicago: University of Chicago Press.

Stark, J. (1994). Should the main goal of statutory drafting be accuracy or clarity. *Statute Law Review*, 15, 207–213.

Stygall, G. (2012). Discourse in the US courtroom. In P. Tiersma and L. Solan, eds., *The Oxford Handbook of Language and Law*. Oxford: Oxford University Press, pp. 369–380.

Thibaut, J. & Walker, L. (1975). *Procedural Justice: A Psychological Analysis*. Hillsdale, NJ: Erlbaum.

Thomas, R. (2012). From 'adversarial v inquisitorial' to 'active, enabling, and investigative': Developments in UK administrative tribunals. In R. Thomas, L. Jacobs and S. Baglay, eds., *The Nature of Inquisitorial Processes in Administrative Regimes: Global Perspectives*. Farnham: Ashgate, pp. 51–70.

Thornborrow, J. (2014). *Power Talk: Language and Interaction in Institutional Discourse*. London: Routledge.

Tickle, L. (2019). 'Sensationalist' 'provocative' and 'unhelpful' – why I was prepared to say in a national newspaper that our state kidnaps children. *Transparency Project*. Accessed 30 May 2023, https://transparencyproject .org.uk/sensationalist-provocative-and-unhelpful-why-i-was-prepared-to-say-in-a-national-newspaper-that-our-state-kidnaps-children/.

Tiersma, P. M. (1999). *Legal Language*. Chicago: University of Chicago Press.

Tiersma, P. (2000). The rocky road to legal reform: Improving the language of jury instructions. *Brooklyn Law Review*, 66(4), 1081–1119.

Tiersma, P. (1993). Linguistic Issues in the Law. *Language*, 69(1), 113–137.

Tiersma, P. & Solan, L. M. (eds.) (2012). *The Oxford Handbook of Language and Law*. Oxford: Oxford University Press.

Tkacukova, T. (2020). Changing landscape of advice provision: Online forums and social media run by McKenzie friends. *Child and Family Law Quarterly*, 4, 397–420.

Tkacukova, T. (2016). Communication in family court: Financial order proceedings from the perspective of litigants in person. *Journal of Social Welfare and Family Law*, 38(4), 430–449.

Tkacukova, T. (2015). A corpus-assisted study of the discourse marker 'well' as an indicator of institutional roles: Professional and lay use in court cases with litigants in person. *Corpora*, 10(2), 145–170.

Tkacukova, T. (2010). Cross-examination questioning: Lay people as cross-examiners. In M. Coulthard and A. Johnson, eds., *The Routledge Handbook of Forensic Linguistics*. London and New York: Routledge, pp. 333–346.

Trinder, L., Hunter, R., Hitchings, E., Miles, J., Moorhead, R., Smith, L., Sefton, M., Hinchly, V., Bader, K. & Pearce, J. (2014). *Litigants in Person in Private Family Law Cases*. Ministry of Justice Analytical Series. www .justice.gov.uk/publications/research-and-analysis/moj

Trinder, L., Firth, A. & Jenks, C. (2010). 'So presumably things have moved on since then?' The management of risk allegations in child contact dispute resolution. *International Journal of Law, Policy and the Family*, 24(1), 29–53.

Tyler, T. (2000). Social justice: outcome and procedure. *International Journal of Psychology*, 35(2), 117–125.

Wagner, A. & Cheng, L. (2011). Language, power and control in courtroom discourse. In A. Wagner and L. Cheng, eds., *Exploring Courtroom Discourse: The Language of Power and Control*. Farnham: Ashgate, pp. 1–10.

Walker, A. G. (1990). Language at work in the law: The customs, conventions, and appellate consequences of court reporting. In J. N. Levi and A. G. Walker, eds., *Language in the Judicial Process*. New York and London: Plenum Press, pp. 203–244.

Walker, A. G. (1986). The verbatim record: The myth and the reality. In S. Fisher and A. D. Todd, eds., *Discourse and Institutional Discourse*. Norwood, NJ: Ablex, pp. 205–222.

Walker, A. G. (1987). Linguistic manipulation, power and the legal setting. In L. Kedar, ed., *Power through Discourse*. Norwood, NJ: Ablex, pp. 57–80.

Wangmann, J., Booth, T. & Kaye, M. (2020). 'No straight lines': Self-represented litigants in family law proceedings involving allegations about family violence (Research report, 24/2020). Sydney: Anrows.

Woodbury, H. (1984). The strategic use of questions in court. *Semiotica*, 48(3–4), 197–228.

Williams, K. (2011). Litigants in person: A literature review. *Research Summary*, 2(11), 355–374.

Wright, D. (2021). Corpus approaches to forensic linguistics. In M. Coulthard, A. May and R. Sousa-Silva, eds., *The Routledge Handbook of Forensic Linguistics*. London: Routledge, pp. 611–627.

Yeung, M. W. & Leung, J. H. (2019). Litigating without speaking legalese: The case of unrepresented litigants in Hong Kong. *International Journal of Speech, Language & the Law*, 26(2), 231–256.

Reports and Procedure Rules

CPR – Rules and Directions. Accessed 30 March 2023. www.justice.gov.uk/courts/procedure-rules/civil/rules.

Children's Experience of Private Family Proceedings: Six key messages from research. 2021. Nuffield Family Justice Observatory. Accessed 30 March 2023. www.nuffieldfjo.org.uk/wp-content/uploads/2021/10/Childrens-experience-of-private-law-proceedings.pdf.

Civil Justice Statistics Quarterly: October to December 2022. (2023). Ministry of Justice. www.gov.uk/government/statistics/civil-justice-statistics-quarterly-october-to-december-2022/civil-justice-statistics-quarterly-october-to-december-2022#defences-including-legal-representation-and-trials.

Courts data. (2023). Accessed 5 April 2023. https://data.justice.gov.uk/courts.

Court statistics for England and Wales. (2023). House of Common Library. https://researchbriefings.files.parliament.uk/documents/CBP-8372/CBP-8372.pdf

Family Court Statistics Quarterly: July to September 2022. www.gov.uk/government/statistics/family-court-statistics-quarterly-july-to-september-2022.

Guidance on 'Financial Needs' on Divorce. (2016). Family Justice Council. www.judiciary.uk/wp-content/uploads/2013/04/guidance-on-financial-needs-on-divorce-june-2016-2.pdf.

HMCTS Reform: Achievements, Challenges and Next Steps. (2023). https://insidehmcts.blog.gov.uk/2023/03/20/hmcts-reform-achievements-challenges-and-next-steps/#comments.

Improving Access to Justice for Separating Families. (2022). JUSTICE. https://justice.org.uk/our-work/civil-justice-system/current-work-civil-justice-system/improving-access-to-justice-for-separating-families/.

Justice Data. (2023). Accessed 21 March 2023. https://data.justice.gov.uk/courts/civil-courts.

Practice Direction 12B – Child Arrangements Programme. Accessed 30 March 2023. www.justice.gov.uk/courts/procedure-rules/family/practice_directions/pd_part_12b.

Litigants in person: Guidelines for lawyers. (2015). The Law Society. www.barcouncilethics.co.uk/documents/litigants-person-guidelines-lawyers/.

Problem-solving courts: An evidence review. (2019). Centre for Justice Innovation. https://justiceinnovation.org/sites/default/files/media/documents/2019-03/problem-solving-courts-an-evidence-review.pdf.

Problem-solving courts: A guide to practice in the United Kingdom. (2023). Centre for Justice Innovation. https://justiceinnovation.org/sites/default/files/media/document/2023/cji_problem-solving-courts-final-0109-web.pdf.

The Family Court Practice (The Red Book). Lexis+ UK. Accessed 30 March 2023. https://plus.lexis.com/uk/document/documentlink/?pdmfid=1001073&crid=3cfce19e-6e24-4768-920b-a3a01f7b8152&pddocfullpath=%2Fshared%2Fdocument%2Fanalytical-materials-uk%2Furn%3AcontentItem%3A8VVF-W5H2-8T41-D4PH-00000-00&pdcontentcomponentid=275417&pdproductcontenttypeid=undefined&pdiskwicview=false&pdpinpoint=&isviewwholeof=true&tocid=urn%3AcontentItem%3A5PFS-46T1-FM2B-W000-00000-00&tocnodeid=AAGAABABFAAQ&doccollection=analytical-materials-uk&hlct=urn%3Ahlct%3A50&pct=urn%3Apct%3A237&docproviderid=-k4k&fonttype=verdana&fontsize=Small&ecomp=-k4k&prid=bcfb059d-8839-4b79-ada5-244322761cde.

Separate Representation of Children. (2006). Department for Constitutional Affairs Consultation Paper, https://dera.ioe.ac.uk/6520/1/cp2006.pdf.

Acknowledgements

I would like to thank Tammy Gales and Tim Grant for guiding me through the process and expressing their support for the project from the very beginning. I am also grateful to the anonymous reviewers for all the insightful comments they offered and the broader questions they posed for further reflection. All this support behind the scenes has undoubtedly helped me improve the final version.

Funding Statement

The research was supported by the Arts and Humanities Research Council Standard Grant AH/S004882/1 'Language of DIY Justice: Communication Practices and Processes'.

Cambridge Elements ☰

Forensic Linguistics

Tim Grant

Aston University

Tim Grant is Professor of Forensic Linguistics, Director of the Aston Institute for Forensic Linguistics, and past president of the International Association of Forensic Linguists. His recent publications have focussed on online sexual abuse conversations including Language and Online Identities: The Undercover Policing of Internet Sexual Crime (with Nicci MacLeod, Cambridge, 2020).

Tim is one of the world's most experienced forensic linguistic practitioners and his case work has involved the analysis of abusive and threatening communications in many different contexts including investigations into sexual assault, stalking, murder, and terrorism. He also makes regular media contributions including presenting police appeals such as for the BBC Crimewatch programme.

Tammy Gales

Hofstra University

Tammy Gales is an Associate Professor of Linguistics and the Director of Research at the Institute for Forensic Linguistics, Threat Assessment, and Strategic Analysis at Hofstra University, New York. She has served on the Executive Committee for the International Association of Forensic Linguists (IAFL), is on the editorial board for the peer-reviewed journals Applied Corpus Linguistics and Language and Law / Linguagem e Direito, and is a member of the advisory board for the BYU Law and Corpus Linguistics group. Her research interests cross the boundaries of forensic linguistics and language and the law, with a primary focus on threatening communications. She has trained law enforcement agents from agencies across Canada and the U.S. and has applied her work to both criminal and civil cases.

About the Series

Elements in Forensic Linguistics provides high-quality accessible writing, bringing cutting-edge forensic linguistics to students and researchers as well as to practitioners in law enforcement and law. Elements in the series range from descriptive linguistics work, documenting a full range of legal and forensic texts and contexts; empirical findings and methodological developments to enhance research, investigative advice, and evidence for courts; and explorations into the theoretical and ethical foundations of research and practice in forensic linguistics.

Cambridge Elements ☰

Forensic Linguistics

Elements in the Series

The Idea of Progress in Forensic Authorship Analysis
Tim Grant

Forensic Linguistics in the Philippines: Origins, Developments, and Directions
Marilu Rañosa-Madrunio and Isabel Pefianco Martin

The Language of Fake News
Jack Grieve and Helena Woodfield

A Theory of Linguistic Individuality for Authorship Analysis
Andrea Nini

Forensic Linguistics in Australia: Origins, Progress and Prospects
Diana Eades, Helen Fraser, and Georgina Heydon

Online Child Sexual Grooming Discourse
Nuria Lorenzo-Dus, Craig Evans, and Ruth Mullineux-Morgan

Spoken Threats from Production to Perception
James Tompkinson

Authorship Analysis in Chinese Social Media Texts
Shaomin Zhang

The Language of Romance Crimes: Interactions of Love, Money, and Threat
Elisabeth Carter

Legal–Lay Discourse and Procedural Justice in Family and County Courts
Tatiana Grieshofer

A full series listing is available at: www.cambridge.org/EIFL

Milton Keynes UK
Ingram Content Group UK Ltd.
UKHW020813080424
440801UK00015B/840